Now You See Me

Make a Great First Impression –
Use the Secrets of Power Networking
for More Clients, More Referrals and
More Friends

2nd Edition, significantly expanded

Tom Marcoux

America's Communication Coach

Spoken Word Strategist

TFG Thought Leader

Speaker-Author of 26 books

Blogger, BeHeardandBeTrusted.com

A QuickBreakthrough Publishing Edition

Other Books by Tom Marcoux:

- Be Heard and Be Trusted: How to Get What You Want
- Nothing Can Stop You This Year!
- Reduce Clutter, Enlarge Your Life
- Darkest Secrets of Persuasion and Seduction Masters
- Darkest Secrets of Charisma
- Darkest Secrets of Negotiation Masters
- Darkest Secrets of the Film and Television Industry Every Actor Should Know
- Darkest Secrets of Making a Pitch to the Film and Television Industry
- Darkest Secrets of Film Directing
- Truth No One Will Tell You

Praise for *Now You See Me* and Tom Marcoux:

• "The powerful and easy-to-use ideas in this book can make a big difference in your business and your personal relationships."
– Allen Klein, author of *You Can't Ruin My Day*

• "As Tom's client for many years, I have benefited from his wisdom and strategic approach. Do your career and personal life a big favor and get his books." – Dr. JoAnn Dahlkoetter, author, *Your Performing Edge* and to CEOs & Olympic Gold Medalists

• "Tom Marcoux has distinguished himself as a coach, speaker and self-help author. His books combine his own philosophy and teachings, as well as those of other success experts, in a highly readable and relatable manner." – Danek S. Kaus, co-author of *Power Persuasion*

Praise for Tom Marcoux's Other Work:

• "In *10 Seconds to Wealth*, Tom Marcoux defines 'the 10 seconds' and on page 2 he reminds us that those all important 10 seconds can come at any time so be prepared. His book focuses on how each of us have divine gifts that we need to understand and use to be our best when those crucial 10 seconds occur. He identifies the divine gifts...love, humility, forgiveness, faith, grace and art and throughout the book shares how these gifts can help us create what we want in our lives, and the wealth we want." – Linda Finkle, author of *Finding The Fork In The Road: The Art of Maximizing the Potential of Business Partnerships*

• "In *Darkest Secrets of Persuasion and Seduction Masters: How to Protect Yourself and Turn the Power to Good*, learn useful countermeasures to protect you from being darkly manipulated."
– David Barron, co-author, *Power Persuasion*

• "In Be Heard and Be Trusted, Tom's advice on how to remain true to yourself and establish authentic rapport with clients is both insightful and reality based. He [shows how] to establish oneself as a credible expert."
- Arthur P. Ciaramicoli, Ed.D., Ph.D., author *The Curse of the Capable*

• "In *Reduce Clutter, Enlarge Your Life*, Marcoux will help you get rid of the physical and mental clutter occupying precious space in your life. You'll reclaim wasted energy, lower your stress, and find time for new opportunities." – Laura Stack, author of *Execution IS the Strategy*

• "In *Power Time Management*, Tom Marcoux shares his extraordinary strategies and methods that save you time, make you money and increase your success and happiness." – Dr. JoAnn Dahlkoetter, author, *Your Performing Edge* and to CEOs & Olympic Gold Medalists

Visit Tom's blog: www.BeHeardandBeTrusted.com

Tom Marcoux

CONTENTS

Dedication and Acknowledgments

Book One: Secrets of Power Networking and Making a 7
Great First Impression

Articles are interspersed in this book . . . by guest
authors Patricia Fripp, Jeanna Gabellini , Randy Gage,
Craig Harrison, C.J. Hayden, and Rebecca Morgan

Book Two: Get More Referrals 51

Book Three: Do Something Better Than Standard 69
Follow Up

Book Four: Create A Great Personal Brand and 83
Enhance Your Power Networking

Book Five: Make a Great First Impression Online 99

Book Six: Become Strong and Enhance Your 111
Networking (includes special Secrets for Introverts)

Book Seven: Put People at Ease: Feel Better through 155
50 METHODS TO SAVE 2 HOURS A DAY

Book Eight: Training Section - Communicate to Win 179

A Final Word; Excerpt from *Darkest Secrets of Persuasion* 225,227
and Seduction Masters: How to Protect Yourself...

About the Author Tom Marcoux, Special Offer Just for 234,236
Readers of this Book

DEDICATION AND ACKNOWLEDGEMENTS

This book is dedicated to the terrific book and film consultant, and author Johanna E. Mac Leod. It is also dedicated to the other team members. Thanks to Barry Adamson II and David MacDowell Blue for editing

Thanks to guest authors Patricia Fripp, Jeanna Gabellini, Randy Gage, Craig Harrison, C.J. Hayden, and Rebecca Morgan. [Their articles remain with their original copyright and are included in this book by their permission.]

Thanks to Judita Bacinskaite rendering this book's front cover. Thank you Johanna E. MacLeod for rendering the back cover. Thanks to my father, Al Marcoux, for his concern and efforts for me. Thanks to my mother, Sumiyo Marcoux, a kind, generous soul. Thank you to Higher Power. Thanks to our readers, audiences, clients, my graduate/college students and my team members of Tom Marcoux Media, LLC. The best to you.

Book One:
Secrets of Power Networking
and Making a Great First Impression

Cheryl's right leg shook. She recognized her symptom of nervousness. "If I don't talk with the guest speaker," she thought, "And I don't introduce myself to other people at this association meeting, I'm just wasting my time and money. I need to take the right action to get more clients. I can do this!" Cheryl took a deep breath. She got on her feet, set her shoulders back, and walked over to the guest speaker and crowd surrounding her.

* * *

Susan looked again at the calendar. Three days left in the month, and she was nine sales away from meeting the department's minimum quota for sales associates.

"I must do better. I need this job," Susan thought, "I know Jonathan and I just met and chatted on Facebook. But he knows Andrea Zhenben who would be a great client for me.

She's a hub of influence. But, what can I do? I don't want to mess this up."

* * *

This next story is about me. I'm writing this book on first impressions, getting more clients and networking because I'm confronted with similar experiences each day.

Some time ago, I gave a presentation to help job seekers at an Employment Development Department workshop.

After the speech, an attendee, Bob, walked up and said to me, "Good speech. You should speak for XY Company."

"Thank you," I responded. Then, using the methods I share in this book, I said three more sentences which led to a meeting and my earning over $250,000.

* * *

The above situations all involve doing well in crucial networking situations.

* * *

Would you like more clients? Have you dreaded trying to make a great first impression when having to meet people in person? Do you get nervous about attending a Chamber of Commerce networking event or an office party?

Have you had concerns about making mistakes on social media?

This book reveals how to develop real confidence so you naturally attract other people and get them to like you. When you learn the skills in this book, you will make great first impressions with greater ease.

This work arises from my over two decades of my own research, personal experience and clients' success stories.

Learn how to ask for referrals and get more leads.

Learn to also avoid the "traps" that people fall into when networking and building a circle of high quality contacts and new business relationships.

Introverts will also find secrets to make good connections.

Expand your networking circle and increase your profits.

We will also cover a *Special Bonus Section* titled **50 Secrets to Save 2 Hours a Day**. When talking with my clients, I have learned that many of them feel stressed out and rushed. I help them with that. Thus, not only will you learn skills for making a good first impression, I also provide you with ways to increase your personal sense of calm and ease.

You will gain the extra benefit of setting yourself at ease as you feel you have *more time* **and** you can set the prospective client at ease. So it's not just about being skillful during a first meeting, it's about how your feel during your workday.

Now, to begin our discussion of networking effectively, I will continue the $250,000 story I started at the beginning of this book. Here is how the dialogue went:

Bob: Great speech. You should speak for ___ Company.

Tom: Thank you. Who should I talk with?

Bob: Her name is Donna S_____.

Tom: Do you have your cell phone with you?

Bob: Yes.

Tom: How about we leave her a voicemail now?

Bob spoke with enthusiasm when he left that voicemail for Donna. It was best to encourage him to leave that message immediately because the next week Bob would have other things on his mind than my speech. It would be too late to use the momentum I had just inspired in Bob. He would not love my speech as much as he did now.

Three days later, I met with Donna. And one week after, I was working with her company.

How to Develop Real Confidence so You Naturally Attract Other People and Get Them to Like You!

Getting People to Like You

(Seven Rapport-Builders to Take the Place of Seven Rapport-Breakers)

Getting people to like you involves building *rapport* which is defined as "a relation characterized by harmony, conformity, accord, or affinity (merriam-webster.com)."

Another facet of the definition of *rapport* is: "confidence of a subject in the operator (as in hypnotism, psychotherapy...), with willingness to cooperate."

To make a great first impression involves having people feel connected to you and a willingness to cooperate.

You can do that by using the below *Seven Rapport-Builders*. The Rapport-Builders replace these rapport-breakers:

1. Talking too much about yourself
2. Appearing awkward, disheveled or disorganized
3. Negative talking (complaining and "poor me" stories)
4. Lacking energy
5. Using a "fake smile"
6. Hesitating (coming across as not confident and not having anything valuable to offer)
7. Dressing inappropriately

The good news is that you develop real confidence when you know how to build rapport. For this, we will use the

C.O.N.N.E.C.T. process:

C – Concentrate on listening
O – Organize your moves and comments
N – Nix the negative stories
N – Nurture your energy
E – Engage by smiling
C – Carry yourself with definite moves
T – Take care with your wardrobe

1. Concentrate on listening
(Overcome "talking too much about yourself")
When you're listening, you're winning. By this I mean, while you are listening, the other person warms up to you. They feel good. We notice there is a great relief felt when you are able to express yourself *and be heard.*

I guide clients to ask gentle questions. It begins with something as simple as: "Hi, I'm ____. And you are?"

Then you can ask another question:
• So how do you know our host Mark?
• So how is the conference going for you?

"Gentle questions" are ones which are easy and often fun to answer. They can include:
• How would I recognize your ideal client?
• What's one of your hobbies?

Start listening and you're building rapport.

2. Organize your moves and comments
(Overcome appearing awkward, disheveled or disorganized)
You have likely met someone who appears awkward and with poor social skills. How did you feel? Uncomfortable. The major idea of making a great first impression is to set

the other person at ease.

We can learn from professional performers as to how to make something look easy. Pop-star Madonna would practice dance moves thousands of times so they would be natural and easy for her.

To look efficient and at ease, actor Arnold Schwarzenegger, in preparation for the feature film *TERMINATOR II,* had a prop rifle next to his desk. All day long he practiced cocking that rifle with one hand. So when the filming day came along, his movements were graceful and with ease.

The same type of dedication can be applied to appearing organized and graceful.

Practice how you will start a conversation.

The easiest way to start is: "Hi, I'm _____ and you are?"

Practice questions for the middle of the conversation.

And practice how you'll end the conversation. For example you could say, "It's been great talking with you. It would be good to stay in contact. Do you have a card?"

If the person does not have a business card, you can pull out a 3x5 card and say, "Oh. I'll make one for you. Are you at gmail or yahoo mail?"

Before you walk into a networking event, go to the restroom and double check your hair (and perhaps, makeup).

Finally, place your business cards somewhere for easy retrieval. It looks awkward for a person to search and search for his or her business cards or pen.

3. Nix the negative stories

(Overcome negative talking, complaining and "poor me" stories)

Do *not* start any conversation complaining about the

traffic or weather. Such talk immediately drains energy from both you and the listener. Instead, pre-plan positive things you can say. When someone asks "So what do you do?" have something pre-planned like: "I help people double their income and triple their time off. I do this through personal coaching and giving presentations. What obstacle is holding you back? Is there something you'd like to do better with your time management?"

You can also pre-plan your positive stories about results your clients have enjoyed.

If the topics in the news come up, be sure to note any good news that has happened recently. You will have to look for it, but someone somewhere has saved a puppy or kitten (for example).

4. Nurture your energy
(Overcome lacking energy)

Come across as "filled with life." How? Get appropriate sleep, good nutrition and daily exercise. There are no shortcuts here. You need to take good care of yourself. It's best to develop helpful patterns. For example, in the car, returning from a restaurant, I will tell my sweetheart, "I'm getting on the treadmill as soon as I get in the house." I make exercise an automatic activity.

5. Engage by smiling
(Overcome using a "fake smile")

Practice smiling. I'm not kidding. Life can be hard and serious. Involve your eyes. Yes, it's natural for little wrinkles to appear around your eyes when you're smiling. It is good to get your face muscles used to having an easy smile. A number of authors suggest that you "take the apples of your checks and have them rise up." Let the smile rise naturally and then flow off your face. People get uncomfortable around those who have a pasted on, fake smile that just "stays there." Confident people smile and then flow into the next moment. A smile conveys warmth and welcome.

6. Carry yourself with definite moves

(Overcome hesitating, that is, appearing as not confident and not having anything valuable to offer)

Be careful to avoid having "stuttering" movements. You have likely seen some people appear socially awkward. Some of them move like a squirrel—stop, start in jerky motions. Avoid that!

Seek to walk with purpose.

With my clients, I invite them to picture a leader or celebrity who moves with power and grace. Years ago, some of my clients pictured a young, strong Sean Connery (as James Bond).

Another technique is to picture yourself standing with great posture as if you had a Superman or Supergirl cape on your shoulders.

Use what works for you.

If you have a tendency to move in fast, jerky motions, replace that with good posture, a smile and moving as if you "owned the place." By the way, "open up" how you gesture with your hands and arms. Years ago, Lynda Obst, producer of *Sleepless in Seattle* (starring Tom Hanks and Meg Ryan) told me, "Take up space."

7. Take care with your wardrobe

(Overcome dressing inappropriately)

Dress like a trusted advisor. Author/Speaker Roger Mellot advised: "Don't try selling tractor equipment while wearing a tuxedo."

For any occasion where you might address the group, dress up a bit. Men do not always have to wear a tie. When I am in Hollywood and meeting with other film industry people, I do *not* wear a tie because I am a film director/producer/screenwriter. I am a "creative" so I do not wear a tie. And yet, I do have my favorite outfit: a deep purple shirt and dark blue suit.

Discover what your good colors are for your wardrobe.

For many of us, warm colors help facilitate a warm connection.

Use the Seven Rapport-Builders:

C – Concentrate on listening

O – Organize your moves and comments

N – Nix the negative stories

N – Nurture your energy

E – Engage by smiling

C – Carry yourself with definite moves

T – Take care with your wardrobe

Then, you will increase your confidence and ability to make a great first impression. Well done!

4 Methods to Increase Your Confidence

We increase our confidence through how we move, dress, and rehearse. We will use the W.I.N.S. process:

W – Walk like a winner

I – Increase rehearsal

N – Nurture "good luck outfits"

S – Start easy

1. Walk like a winner

The way you move can change how you feel. Some

people move like a squirrel with darting, nervous moves (as I mentioned before). No wonder they feel frantic.

The solution is to "walk like a winner." Our feelings often follow how we move physically. Let's do an experiment. Slump over in your chair. Round your shoulders downward. Do you feel a bit down? That is natural.

Now, sit up straight and tall. Better yet—stand up. Now, fill your chest with air and hold your shoulders back as if you had a superhero cape flowing from your shoulders. Do you feel stronger? Great! This is how a confident person stands and walks. The fastest, easiest way to increase your confidence is to move in a way a confident person moves.

I don't sing because I'm happy; I'm happy because I sing.
- William James

Will you place posted notes around your home to remind yourself to practice the walk and posture of a winner?

2. Increase rehearsal

To integrate new behaviors into our lives, rehearsal forms a crucial element in our journey. Before any presentation, I rehearse new material with a friend, family member or, at least, with an audio recorder. When I turn on my audio recorder, I feel like I am "on stage." It really helps.

What would you like to rehearse? Your opening lines? How you walk across a room?

3. Nurture "good luck outfits"

Lynda Obst, producer of *Contact* (starring Jodie Foster), told me: "In the beginning, I had good luck outfits for important meetings."

Pick clothing that makes you feel better and stronger.

With clothing, choose colors that work for you. Warm colors create a warm first impression. Since I discovered red works for me, I have worn a red shirt as a lead character in two feature films (one I directed went to the Cannes film market).

What colors work for you? What warm colors work for you? Which ones do you prefer?

4. Start easy

To begin practicing new techniques, it helps to start with something easy. For example, author Ginnie Sales teaches people how to flirt. She told me how she became comfortable in starting up conversations with strangers: Ginnie *started easy* by talking with mothers who had children with them in the supermarket.

Start practicing your skills in starting conversations by engaging people whom you feel would cause the least amount of stress and anxiety.

Who do you feel you can easily approach for starting a conversation?

How to Get People to Like You

People do business with people whom they like and trust. We will use the L.I.K.E.-M.E.-N.O.W. process (which I introduced in my book *Be Heard and Be Trusted*, 3rd Edition):

L - Listen
I - Interview
K – Kindle similarity
E – Express gratitude
M – Monitor time
E – Engage the person's concerns
N – Note ideal clients

O – Open to humor
W – Watch and help

1. Listen
Listen first. Ask a gentle questions like: "So how do you know our host, Matt?"

2. Interview
Imagine that you are conducting a friendly interview. I often ask, "What's one of your hobbies?" A significant number of people prefer to talk about a hobby because they may not enjoy their current job. You might ask, "What are you looking forward to?"

3. Kindle similarity
A conversation warms up when people have a "Me, too!" moment. You often hear a comment like: "Oh, you like skiing, too? What's one of your favorite resorts?"

4. Express gratitude
You can say, "Thanks for your time" or "Thanks for your efforts on this one." In an email, it often helps to begin with "Thank you for . . ."

5. Monitor time
Respect the person's time. Say things like: "This will be quick. I know you're busy."

6. Engage the person's concerns
Ask gentle questions to find out what is causing pain or inconvenience for the person. Then you can show how you hold similar concerns. This creates connection. Be careful to hear the person out. You can ask, "Anything else?" When

you reply with, "I can relate to that because," be careful to avoid going "one up." To one up is to say something like: "Oh, you have a newborn baby. That's tough. I have newborn twins." *Instead,* be sure to keep the focus on the other person's concerns.

7. Note ideal clients

Ask, "Who's your ideal client?" Then continue with: "How would I recognize them? . . . I'll see if I can send some people your way."

8. Open to humor

Appropriate humor can warm up a conversation. However, we need to be careful about humor. Avoid putting down anyone. You can point out a harmless error you may have done. With such self-deprecating humor, avoid saying anything that implies that you are incompetent.

Humor is important, and I shared 30 Secrets of Humor in my book *10 Seconds to Wealth.* Observe what the other person finds funny and seek to flow with it.

"Among those whom I like or admire, I can find no common denominator, but among those whom I love, I can: all of them make me laugh." - W. H. Auden

9. Watch and help

Ask, "How can I be supportive of what you're doing?" Avoid the tired "How can I help you?" It causes many people to recoil because they have heard it from certain insincere sales clerks.

When a person tells you about how you can be supportive, give yourself time to think about it. (I call this "thinkspace.") You can reply, "Let me double check a couple of things and see how I might help. How about I get back to you on Thursday afternoon?"

How the Experience of True Confidence Can Help You Make a Great First Impression

When my clients take action from the experience of true confidence, they enjoy a freedom they did not expect.

Many of us are *hoping for the moment of confidence and comfort* when it's simply easy to do something difficult, scary, or even perhaps painful.

Don't wait.

Every successful person I have interviewed has said something that can be summed up with these words:

- I was scared, but I did it anyway.
- No, I didn't feel comfortable, but I wanted it so much that I took the risk.
- Yes, I was afraid, but I stretched; I tried something new.

Confidence is *not* comfort.

It's something else.

Confidence is a *knowing* that you will, in any situation, adapt, learn and be flexible.

In other words, confidence is knowing you are competent in the skills of adapting, learning and being flexible in the moment. Such skills can be learned and practiced.

For my clients to easily remember the above ideas, I reduce them to "A.L.F. – adapt, learn, flex."

Here is the great news: You can train and prepare and rehearse so that in the critical moment you are better able to adapt, learn, and be flexible—and things will turn out well.

When I taught workshops to MBA students at Stanford University, I was pleased with a number of details of my teaching performance. However, just today, I had a *new insight* to something that I could have done differently.

If I gave another workshop tomorrow, I would probably start the class with the students forming a half-circle of chairs.

I would sit in a chair, and I might say,

"Thank you for attending this workshop. I'm excited and glad to work with you. Now, we'll begin with a conversation.

When I teach graduate students, I usually have 15 weeks to explore with and serve the students.

Today, we have this *one session.*

So I invite you to join me and *together,* we'll make this session *relevant to your life*—to the people in *this* room.

So about making a great first impression, what are you concerned about? What bothers you? What are you afraid of?

[Silence.]

Ahhh. It's quiet. We're thinking. That's good [I'm smiling.]

Okay. I'll start. What am I afraid of? I'm afraid some of you may have tuned out. That's okay. I'm ready.

How many of you are concerned about getting access to the hidden job market?

[Hands go up]

Good. I have five proven steps to help you with that.

I've got methods *backed up by research.* Backed up by *success stories of my clients.* And personal experience. I have four sentences that took me from a first impression to making thousands of dollars. Still, I'm going to write on this board what **you're** most concerned about.

So we have one thing. [I write down "Access to hidden job market."] Many of you just told me that you want to access the hidden job market. Now, we're cooking!"

My point with sharing with you the above workshop example is that top professionals keep learning, keep adapting, and keep responding in this present moment.

For example, the above speech, I *rehearsed today* prior to

typing it here. And I'm not scheduled for Stanford University again [not yet].

My confidence as a speaker comes from A.L.F. (adapt, learn, flex)—*not from waiting* for that moment when I am comfortable.

I am going to add one more detail to A.L.F. Think of it as "ALFS."

"S" stands for "Secure help."

How do I continually build my confidence as a speaker (member of National Speakers Association for fourteen years)?

I secure help from the audience to guide me in how to serve them well. I make my presentation a dialogue.

I secure help from my own mentors and coaches.

I secure help from my test audiences before I give my speeches.

You get the idea.

So I invite you to connect with the source of True Confidence: ALFS

A – Adapt

L – Learn

F – Flex

S – Secure help

Take action.

Courage is easier when you're prepared.

Rehearse.

Be genuine in the moment.

So how does True Confidence help you make a Great First Impression? When you practice the skills of ALFS, you feel stronger and ready to adapt to any conversation with a new person.

As I mentioned, your true confidence is *not* built on a fleeting feeling of comfort. No. It is built on *your knowing that you will adapt in the moment.*

Rehearsal is key. Think of how rehearsal keeps a dancer flexible. And . . .

You need preparation so you're strong to face the unknowns.

While it may be true that you can feel more comfortable over time by practicing certain skills like a golf swing. DO NOT WAIT for feeling comfortable before you take action.

In a sense, confidence is about ALFS skills. Become competent in ALFS skills.

Practicing ALFS skills will help you feel stronger.

I know this to be true because I started off as a shy, terrified boy playing piano for 31 seniors in a retirement home. I *still* have some introvert tendencies.

So I searched for the truth about confidence and for being able to face tough moments with poise. Thus, I developed ALFS to help myself and my clients overcome tendencies that may limit success.

The best to you on your journey.

A Confident Person is Not Ruffled by a Mistake: 2 Methods to Easily Recover from Any Conversation Mistake

Want to eliminate hesitation when you're about to talk with new people? Learn to pre-plan graceful ways to overcome a conversation mistake.

Method #1: Use the phrase, "That's not what I meant to say. What I meant to say is . . .."

If you say something that comes out in a way that you do not like, you can immediately say: "That's not what I meant to say. What I meant to say is. . ." Practice this phrase. Say it out loud now. Reading is not enough. You need to practice expressing it aloud. Then it becomes easy.

Method #2: Use the phrase "Forgive me, I was just . . ."
When you say, "I'm sorry," you express your regret. However, when you say, "Forgive me," you invite the other person to take action. You ask for the person's participation.

Author Marshall Sylver notes that a salesperson can say something like: *"Forgive me, I was just* so excited about how you'll enjoy feeling the power of this car."

Note a phrase that you would feel comfortable saying.

Make A Great First Impression At an In-person Networking Event:

Four Methods to Make Time for Yourself to Feel Refreshed <u>Before</u> the Networking Event

Making a great first impression at an in-person networking event begins *before* the event. It is about feeling refreshed and energized. Then you will have lively energy visible on your face. So we will use the F.A.C.E. process:

F – Free time by saying "no"

A – Arrange help

C – Combine activities

E – Encourage trading tasks

1. Free time by saying "no
Cynthia complained to two friends that she felt overwhelmed. The problem was Cynthia so desperately craved approval she said *yes* too quickly to requests.

Her friends knew this and sometimes suggested to each other, "Why don't you ask Cynthia to help you with that?

She helps everybody."

One way to free yourself from feeling overwhelmed is to learn how to effectively and gracefully say *no*. Here are some notes on saying no. This is a complicated issue. The words we use vary upon our personal style, the other person's style and the situation *in the moment*. Here are some notes on saying *no*:

1) *Take care your own feelings, and you will have the energy to be good to others.* My coaching clients have mentioned how they eventually "lash out" with an irritable remark when they have gone through a period of over-accommodating others—ignoring themselves. So we have a choice: a) say *no* at times, or b) erupt like a volcano later. You can say, "I'll have to say no at this time. My plate is full. I'm making sure I don't get overwhelmed..."

2) *Remind yourself that saying 'no' does not cause someone to feel hurt.* It just sets up a situation for the person to choose her reaction or response. Ultimately, it is up to her when she decides to "move on from feeling upset" about a situation. She might even simply say, "Okay. I'll look for another way to get this done."

When you need to say *no* (in order to say *yes* to yourself for something else), you can choose to help the person find an alternative. You might say something like:

"Thanks for thinking of me. I'll have to say *no* at this time. Perhaps, I can help you brainstorm about someone who might be able to help you with that."

You could even say something like: "Forgive me, I unfortunately cannot help right now, but I might be able to help you find someone who can. Who do you know who might be able to help you accomplish that task?"

3) Remember your first responsibility is to yourself. I remember one time I was vacationing with a friend. He chose not to eat breakfast, and he chose to wait for me. I had a number of time-urgent tasks to do that morning. Later, my friend was upset. Part of my response was, "I'm concerned that you feel uncomfortable. Please do what you need to do to feel comfortable."

This interchange flowed in a new direction away from my friend trying to blame me for how his stomach felt. Later, we planned times for when we would go our separate ways and then later meet up. When interacting with adults (children are a different story), we can create a space in which individuals take care of their own personal needs.

4) Stay open to accepting your uncomfortable feeling around saying "no." In the above "breakfast example," my first response was to feel bad that my friend was hurting. I said, "Please do what you need to do to feel comfortable," to remind *myself* that my friend had made his *own* decision to wait.

How you can effectively say *no:*

a) Learn to say *no* graciously. You can say, "Thank you for asking . . . Thank you for thinking of me . . ."

b) Say *no* as soon as possible to give the other person notice.

c) Acknowledge the other person's feelings.

d) Acknowledge any error you may have made like not calling back earlier.

e) Decide if you want to help the person look for alternative solutions.

f) Accept the times when the other people choose (on some level) to remain in a "hurt" mood.

g) Decide if it is appropriate to "make it up" to the person —perhaps, with a small gift.

h) Stay open to accepting your own uncomfortable feelings around saying *no.*

i) Stay in contact with the person. You may decide to let the other person cool off for a day or more. Then touch base with him or her.

The above ideas are like a menu. Try some of them and see what works for you. From a spiritual point of view, it helps when we remember: "My Spirit is bigger than my current uncomfortable feeling. I can chose to focus on my Spirit."

Do you feel overwhelmed? What methods would you like to try for saying "no" gracefully?

2. Arrange help

Many times, we hesitate to spend money on getting help because we are concerned about our personal finances. This is quite understandable. Still we can open our perspective to the idea that we "invest" in ourselves when we invest in getting help or assistance. For example, one of my friends invested $35.00 a month in having a gardener take care of her yard and front lawn. It was a great investment in that she could do other things (including tasks of her own business).

Perhaps, you might hire a trustworthy high school student to assist you with emptying your garage. Realize that we can make more money, but we cannot replace the time of our life.

For what tasks would you like to hire inexpensive help?

3. Combine Activities

If you need to return phone calls to friends, you can ride a stationary bicycle (or use a treadmill) at the same time. Ask your friend in advance if they are okay with talking with you when your breathing may sound a bit strained.

Further, you can watch a favorite sit-com and safely use your exercise equipment simultaneously.

What activities can you combine to get double the value for your time?

4. Encourage trading tasks

Often, we can get more done when we trade tasks with a friend. One time, I helped a friend by typing up his term paper. At the time, I typed at over 73 words a minute, so he saved time. In return, he helped me with editing one of my film projects.

Note two friends and two tasks that you might trade with them.

At the Networking Event –
Five Methods to Create Instant Rapport

Rapport is defined as "relation characterized by harmony, conformity, accord, or affinity" (merriam-webster.com).

Gaining rapport helps us make a warm connection that can lead to opportunities and even friendships.

When I give a presentation on "First Impressions Are Everything: Break the 3-Second Barrier and Influence People," I identify the 3-Second Barrier as a wall that people put up based on the quick judgments made about a new person.

These judgments can include:
• Good dresser
• Sour face

- Friendly face
- Hesitant in saying hello: here's an aloof person
- Hesitant in saying hello: here's a person with no self-confidence who probably has nothing to offer.

To beat the 3-second Barrier, we need to learn and practice effective methods of communication that I share throughout this book.

We want the judgments created in the first 3 seconds, 30 seconds, five minutes and beyond to be judgments that *open the door* to a new friendship.

To gain rapport quickly, we will use the S.M.I.L.E. process:

S - Smile
M – Mirror verbal/body language
I - Inquire
L - Listen
E – Engage to her positive past

1. Smile

Some researchers suggest that a communication from one person has 58% of its impact in one's facial expression.

Others may disagree with the actual percentage, but all agree that facial expressions are important.

Further research shows that people respond positively to genuine smiles. This is why I mention to my clients "smile as you flow in the moment." By this I mean, smile in a natural way: let the smile flow onto your face and then, when appropriate, gently flow off.

This is the opposite of the mistaken, pasted-on smile.

People who are confident are those who are alive in the moment. If something is really amusing, they smile. But confident people *avoid* the sickly, ingratiating smile. No pasted-on smiles for successful, confident people.

In a room when you're alone, you might need to warm up your smiling muscles. I remember the old story of a little girl seeing a frown on her father's face. "Dad, are you angry?" she asked.

"No, I feel fine," he replied.

She said, "Then, tell your face!"

2. Mirror verbal/body language

People feel rapport with another person when they perceive some form of similarity. You can accomplish a form of similarity by matching or "mirroring" the other person's physical behavior.

For example, if you're talking with an extrovert who uses her hands in wide-open gestures, you can occasionally open your gestures wider. I use the word *occasionally* with care because I once saw "mirroring" backfire. Someone was mirroring every gesture I was doing. I noticed this and felt like the person was being manipulative. This severed rapport. Let your mirroring be subtle. By the way, wait at least twenty seconds before you move to have a similar posture as another person.

About mirroring verbal habits: If you're talking with a slow-talking person, you might want to slow down your words if you tend to talk rapidly. If you're talking with a soft-spoken person, you might find it helpful to lower your own voice.

What would help you feel comfortable in "mirroring" the person's verbal or behavioral habits?

3. Inquire

Ask uplifting questions. By this I mean, ask something that places the person into a good mood.

Here are examples of such questions:

- What are you looking forward to?
- Who is your ideal client?
- What's next for you?
- What's one of your hobbies?
- What 's one of your favorite movies or books?

Name two uplifting questions you will use in your next first encounter with a new person.

4. Listen

The fastest way to create rapport and trust is listening to the person as soon as possible. This is why I emphasize: When you're listening, you're winning. When the other person feels special, he or she naturally wants to cooperate with you.

Every person wants to be heard. The rapid way to begin listening is to ask a "gentle question" (meaning, a question that is easy and, perhaps, fun to answer). When I meet a new person, I often say, "Hello, I'm Tom and you are—?"

After the person answers my first question, I can easily flow to another question like: "How do you know Mark, our host?" or "Are you looking forward to a particular speaker at this conference?"

What questions do you feel comfortable in asking?

5. Engage to her positive past

One way to help a person feel good about us is to guide the person to talk about something positive from *his or her own past*. Help the person express details about a moment in the past when he or she was feeling great. You can help the person remember a fun time by saying, "Tell me about an event that you really enjoyed."

Here is an advanced technique: While you see the person smile as he is talking about a fun, past moment, you can touch his forearm and say something like: "It feels *great*, talking with you about this." *WARNING: This technique requires expert-timing and confidence.* The benefit of this technique is: you are linking your presence to the person's good feelings. [Such linking is called "anchoring" in Neuro-linguistic Programming circles.]

Why would someone want to practice the "Touch the forearm during positive memory" technique? Research shows that people tend to buy more from people who touch their arm. For example, restaurant-goers provide a higher tip to a server who touches their forearm.

With whom can you practice getting another person to recall a positive moment from his or her past?

At the Networking Event
Four Methods to Increase Your Comfort

When we are stretching, it's helpful to have some forms of comfort or even having a way to recharge along the way. We will use the I.C.A.N. process:

I – Increase energy before
C – Comfort yourself along the way
A – Act like a host
N – Nurture a small goal

1. Increase energy before

Some introverts find themselves dreading the necessity to go to a networking event. One important factor is: How we feel is often based on our personal energy. It might be best to cancel any meetings before the event so the introvert can reserve his or her personal energy for the event. Also, the introvert might want to grab a "power nap" (often 20 minutes) before the networking event.

2. Comfort yourself along the way

Comforting yourself could be simply taking a drink of water between conversations.

Another way to gain comfort is bringing an upbeat friend with you to the event. Your friend can act like a coach and say encouraging words like: "Come on Sandy, you're ready to meet that guy over there. Go over. Ask him: 'So how do you know Bob and Janet?'"

After you have a conversation with a new person, you can return to your friend for more encouragement and a boost to your energy. This will likely increase your resolve to speak to the next new person.

Name two possible upbeat friends to take to the next networking event.

3. Act like a host

We often feel more comfortable when we are "playing a role." Susan RoAnne, author of *How to Work a Room*, told me that she will often "play the hostess." She walks into a room where she knows no one, picks up a bowl of chips, and walks around offering the chips. This process helps her begin conversations.

How can you comfortably play a role at the next event you want to attend?

4. Nurture a small goal

Perhaps you'd like to begin with a small goal like: "Meet the host and ask her to introduce me to two new people." Every little step counts. We never know what contact will bring a new adventure into our life. For example, I showed a screenplay to a software engineer and then . . .

- The script went to another software engineer
- The script was passed to a real estate developer
- The script ended in the hands of the California Motion Picture Commissioner

The California Motion Picture Commissioner then helped me secure San Luis Obispo Airport (this was before the Sept. 11th Tragedies) and an American Eagle airplane for *free.*

For a networking event, a smart goal might be have ten good conversations. Also, if you have introvert tendencies, you might set the goal of networking for one hour, fifteen minutes. Just having a planned, short duration at the event can help an introvert feel resilient enough to attend the networking event.

I admit that whenever my sweetheart mentions some social occasion my first question is usually, "How long is it?" My reason is that I feel "on stage" at any social event.

Making a great first impression requires significant personal energy.

Use the I.C.A.N. process:

I – Increase energy before

C – Comfort yourself along the way

A – Act like a host

N – Nurture a small goal

The best to you at your next networking event.

How to Take Your Great First Impression to the Next Level:

Make It Easy for Them to Say Yes

For many of us, the real value of networking is to have a number of people say "yes" to us.

How would your life be better if someone said yes to you?

My clients want people to say *yes* for

- More sales
- More friendships
- More opportunities
- More assistance with tough situations

We will use the E.A.S.Y. process to help other people feel it's *easy* to say yes to us.

E – Establish trust

A – Ask

S – Serve ahead of time ("Do the work for them")

Y – Yearn for ease

1. Establish trust

How do you know if you can trust someone?

Think about a friend you trust. What were the details that made you certain that your friend cares about you?

I will give you a strong example. It is likely that my interest in effective communication began as I saw and endured the communication mistakes my father made and continues to make.

First thing, my father simply does not listen to family members. Here is the truth: I do not trust my father to care about what is important to me. Why? He does not listen. Now, nearly 80 years old he is consumed with his own bitterness. When I visit my parents I have no idea if my father will duck out or have harsh words for me.

So my point here is: **Establish trust by listening well to the other person.**

Invite the other person to talk by asking gentle questions (a question that is easy to answer and perhaps even fun to answer).

I have shared these questions earlier:

- What are you looking forward to?
- Who is your ideal client?
- What's next for you?
- What's one of your hobbies?
- What 's one of your favorite movies or books?
- How are things going?

Then provide what I call *Reflective Replies*. You reflect to the person (as if you are a mirror) his or her feelings. Here are sample Reflective Replies:
- That sounds frustrating. Then what happened?
- That sounds disappointing. How did you want things to improve?

Avoid saying, "You sound angry." A lot of people think that "being angry" is equal to "being out of control." So they feel insulted.

Instead, you can say things like "frustrating, painful, or irritating." Let the other person decide to say whether he or she was angry—or not.

And then, ask an *interested-follow up question* like:
- That sounds important. So what did you say to Joe then?
- That sounds like a turning point. What did you want Mary to understand at that time?

Listening well is *not* just keeping your mouth shut. It is demonstrating that you understand. Express what you heard with something like:

"I hear you to say _____. Do I have that about right?"

After you ask that question, the person has the chance to confirm or adjust the information until she feels you really understand her feelings and thoughts on the matter. When that happens, it's easier to get her cooperation for something that you suggest.

2. Ask

When you ask for something, make it easy and simple for the person to respond positively. Do NOT ask for too much. Ask for one thing. Or better yet, ask for "this or that."

One time a vendor caused a big problem for a family member. I said, "How about you solve this quickly. You could do XY or you could do 1-2-3."

When you ask for something, be sure to leave the person a "graceful out." No one likes to be pressed against a wall.

You can say:

- "It would be great if you could do _____. I'd really appreciate it. I understand that you're busy. So if it's not possible at this time . . ."
- "It would be great if you could endorse my book. I realize that it might not be your cup of tea. So we could do something else if you prefer."

3. Serve ahead of time ("Do the work for them.")

Do the work for them relates to "doing your homework."

If you have a presentation for a potential client, come up with "10 Worst Questions You Don't Want to Answer." Then come up with two answers per question. Now you're "armed" with 20 answers!

During the presentation you could even "handle the objection proactively." By this I mean, you could say something like: "I've had a couple of clients who had a concern about how long it would take for their employees to learn the system. To make it faster and easier, we have this 1-2-3 schedule and . . ."

If you want someone to write an endorsement for you, you could say, "I'll listen to you and write up a rough draft.

Would that help make it easier and faster for you?"

Make it easy for the person. Go to her office.

Write the rough draft. Offer to talk with her staff if background information is needed.

A number of people want to be helpful, but they are pressed for time and they have little energy. So you do the work for them.

4. Yearn for ease

When I say, "yearn for ease," I'm talking about making "ease" a priority. Look at the situation from the other person's point of view.

It took time for me to learn to make "ease" a priority. When I first made films, I was a "good soldier." It was likely because my father (a former Marine and former Air Force man) instilled discipline in me. He gave me two books: *The Samurai* and *Bushido*. Both books emphasized discipline and self-sacrifice.

As I made more films, I learned that a number of people are not looking for discipline or "jumping on the grenade to save your fellow soldiers." They were looking for the easy way out.

I adjusted my leadership tactics. I made sure when talking with a person that they could clearly see what was in it for them. I also demonstrated how following my plan, they would have an easier path.

So make ease for the other person a priority. More often, you will get the *yes* you want.

* * *

Now, we will learn about more networking methods from Craig Harrison.

Is Networking *Not* Working For You?
9 Mistakes Networkers Make and
26 Tips for Networking Success
by Craig Harrison

I attend a variety of networking events and marvel and the basic and banal mistakes I see would-be networkers making. It was enough to make me want to write this article for my colleague in communication, Tom Marcoux.

Tom and I agree, Networking is about meeting new people, letting them meet you, and prospecting for jobs, contracts, clients and more. Effective networking expands your circle of contacts, and by extension, your sphere of influence. Ineffective networking tires you out and discourages you by its lack of productivity. Worse yet, on occasion, you can actually leave a bad impression with strangers. Beware the following networking mistakes.

Bad networkers mumble. A mumble is a speaking stumble, people mumble their name, their occupation and their titles all the time. Your name is irrelevant if we can't hear it. You've been saying your name all your life so you may be bored with it, yet we may only hear it once. State your name clearly, slowly and in a way someone can repeat and remember it. It's your lifeline to contact. Take care in stating it.

Poor networkers don't emphasize the benefits, but usually the features of what they do. Too many job seekers focus on the features of their work instead of the end-results. Employers buy benefits, solutions and outcomes. Speak their language by focusing on what you can do for them, not how you do it. Example: project managers help companies save time and money (two benefits/outcomes) through expertly managing projects and people (features).

Monotonal delivery. If you can't convey your qualifications, passion and employability in 30 seconds you may not get 30 minutes in an interview. Use vocal variety, intonation and enthusiasm to speak confidently about yourself, others. (Toastmasters www.toastmasters.org* can help you improve your conversational voice.)

Shpiel too long. Networking is not speechmaking. You have a finite window of opportunity to introduce yourself and glean a few details about the person you're talking to. You can't recite your resume, tell your life story or otherwise drone on. Keep it short and sweet!

Unfocused conversation. Networking is a chance to demonstrate focus, drive and confidence. Aimless rambling is pointless, and suggests you're not a focused professional. Showcase your communication skills by expressing yourself succinctly and ask precise questions.

Leakage. Is there is an inconsistency between what you say and what you do? Your card may say one thing about you, your clothing suggests something else and the language and vocabulary you use further confounds strangers in getting a fix on who you are, what you are about and your skill level. Strive to send consistent messages verbally, non-verbally and in your materials and correspondence. When everything works together the sum is greater than its parts.

You don't mind your manners. Poor Networkers can't make small talk, don't show an ability to exchange pleasantries, and often interrupt others. Can you gracefully engage and disengage from conversations? Are your questions intrusive and your answers curt? Are you showing proper respect for the stranger you've just met? Or are you singing Opera? If so, your tune is familiar: It's "Me-Me-Me-Me-Me!"

Slinging Slang. Many networkers profess to have

excellent communication skills yet use slang or mispronounce big words when little words are better. Beware the use of contractions, excessive acronyms and name-dropping too. Don't tell us what you're gonna do! I would like to hear what you are going to do instead.

Disrespect the Tao of Networking. Networkers who are obsequious to those they believe can help them, yet rude to those they believe can't help them, disrespect networking. I've had networkers disparage the last person they met while in conversation with me. I was afraid to let them go for fear of what they would next say about me! That's antithetical to the spirit of networking. One networker took my card and, in front of me, wrote the letter A on it, and boasted he was "putting me in his A list." Let's just say he was clearly the biggest A I met that night!

Networking From A to Z

Arrive early for best results
Be a good listener
Clearly enunciate (your name, your words, your sentences…)
Don't interrupt
Exude confidence in your communication and how you carry yourself
Focus on your conversational partner (not those around him or her)
Gather information about your conversational partner
Help your listener remember you by what you say and how you say it
Inquire about them!
Jump-start conversations with questions, compliments or provocative statements

Know or learn how you can best help others

Listen actively (through the use of using gestures, facial expressions, body language, verbal utterances, etc.)

Make and keep eye contact

Never stare or crowd your conversational party...respect their personal space.

Open-ended questions generate valuable insights

Presentation skills matter!

Questions keep your dialog going. When it stalls, ask more.

Respect others' time by being focused.

Study non-verbal cues of your listener: do they agree, care, understand?

Think before you speak.

Uncover their needs, pain, problems that you can solve.

Value their time by not monopolizing it.

Write a thank-you note or e-mail to follow up with strangers you meet.

X is a variable whose value is unknown. Get to know others to appreciate their true value.

You are unique. Showcase your uniqueness through your style, what you say and do.

Zzzzzz. What they'll do if you can't keep 'em awake with mutually beneficial conversation!

Craig Harrison's ExpressionsOfExcellence.com provides sales and service solutions for organizations and communication and leadership development for individuals. Based in the San Francisco Bay Area, Craig is a speaker, trainer, author, consultant, coach and storyteller and an active leader in the National Speakers Association, Toastmasters International and National Storytelling Network

* Download Craig's free Quick Start Guide to finding the best Toastmasters club for you!

www.ExpressionsOfExcellence.com/Toastmasters/QuickStartG
uide_Toastmasters.pdf

* * *

Now, we will learn from Rebecca Morgan's insights related to networking and getting along well with people.

Trying to Be the Smartest in the Room Shows You're Not
by Rebecca Morgan, CSP, CMC

Recently I spent a few days with a young, bright woman. But her constant attempts to prove she was the smartest person in the room backfired. The more she tried to one-up others, the less smart she was seen to be.

I empathized because at her age I, too, suffered from the same low self-esteem that caused me to try to show anyone who'd listen how smart I was. I guess I didn't believe enough in my own capabilities to be at peace. I felt an urge to try to put others in their place so I could appear to come out on top. And I would argue about nearly every statement mostly just to show I was a critical thinker.

But over time, I saw that if one was constantly argumentative and cantankerous to try to get others to see one's superior (?) logic and intellect, it really showed one had less of both.

This young woman would make broad generalizations about many groups: "All men just want…" "(An ethnic group) are really lazy." "Californians are…" She had strong opinions and generalizations about those belonging to each political party, profession, sexual orientation, nationality, etc. When someone would push back and say, "Some

Californians are like that, but not all." She'd argue why her opinion was right.

This grows wearisome. So much so she was hard to be around. She would spew forth "facts" she'd heard from some commentator on cable news programs without realizing this was opinion, not fact. She'd share findings from "research" which was really surveying people's point of view.

She didn't realize she'd garner more respect if she said, "I've found some (Californians, men, etc.) can..." Or, "I heard an interesting commentator sharing his ideas about..." Or, "I've noticed that.... What's your experience (or opinion) regarding that?" By being interested in other's perspective, you show you don't believe you have all the answers.

Rebecca L. Morgan, CSP, CMC, specializes in creating innovative solutions for customer service challenges. She's appeared on *60 Minutes, Oprah, the Wall Street Journal, National Public Radio* and *USA Today*. Rebecca is the bestselling author of 25 books, including *Calming Upset Customers* and *Professional Selling*. She is an exemplary resource who partners with you to accomplish high ROI on your strategic customer service projects. For information on her services, books, and resources, or for permission to repost or reprint this article, contact her at 408/998-7977, Rebecca@RebeccaMorgan.com, http://www.RebeccaMorgan.com/

* * *

Now, we will learn C.J. Hayden's insights about effectively networking and marketing. Her comments might surprise you in a truly helpful way.

Not Enough Clients? What's In Your Way?
by C.J. Hayden, MCC, CPCC

What's stopping you from getting all the clients you want? Do you know? The answer to this one question may be the key to making your marketing more successful.

It would seem from the questions people ask me about marketing that everyone is trying to fix just one type of problem—how to fill their marketing pipeline with more new prospects.

"What else should I be doing to attract potential clients?" they ask. "Where else can I go to find people who might hire me?" or "How can I be more visible online so people will contact me?" or "Should I be finding prospects by cold calling, using Twitter, running ads, giving talks, writing articles…?"

All their questions--and it seems all their efforts--are aimed at finding ways to make contact with new people who might become clients. And every time they identify another activity that might help their pipeline get fuller, they want to add it to their ever-growing to-do list.

But is this really what's stopping them from getting more clients? Is this what's stopping you? If you are already marketing yourself in four or five different ways, will increasing that to seven or eight different ways produce better results? Or alternatively, if you drop everything you're doing now, and start using four or five brand new marketing approaches, will that do the trick?

In my experience, it probably won't. Continuing to try new and different approaches to fill your marketing pipeline will more often result in overwhelm, wasted effort, and failure than it will in new clients.

Instead of trying to fix your marketing by just seeking out more ways to meet people or collect names, email addresses and phone numbers, stop for a moment. What is the problem you're trying to solve? In other words, what's really getting in the way of your marketing success?

Listed below are the five most common marketing problems, and questions to ask yourself to see which ones might be yours. They're presented in order of priority— problem #1 needs to be fixed before tackling problem #2, and so on. Consider whether making changes in one of these areas might be exactly the fix your marketing needs.

1. HANDS-ON TIME: Are you spending enough time proactively marketing? Not just getting ready to market, or thinking about how to market, or feeling resistant to marketing, but actually taking steps that will lead directly to landing clients?

If you're not spending enough time marketing your business, fixing other problem areas won't help much. Start keeping track of how much time you spend actively marketing each week. Most independent professionals find they need to spend from 4-16 hours weekly—less when you're busy with paying work; more when you're not.

2. TARGET MARKET: Do you have a clearly defined target market which you can describe in five words or less? Does this market already know they need your services? And are you spending most of your time marketing to exactly that group?

Once you feel confident you are dedicating enough time to marketing, the next hurdle is making sure you're marketing to the right people. Focusing your efforts on a specific target group with a defined need for your services will make everything you do more effective.

3. MARKETING MESSAGE: Do your descriptions of your services name the benefits you offer and results you produce for your target market? And are these benefits and results that this market is looking for? Do you deliver your message every time you make contact?

Letting prospective clients know exactly how you can help them will make the most of the time you spend marketing to a defined audience. Your message needs to be clear, focused on the client's needs, and typically delivered multiple times to the same prospects.

4. FOLLOW-THROUGH: Do you have a system for following up with every prospect until they say either yes or no? Are you able to complete all the steps for each marketing approach you are using to make it pay off?

Without follow-through, much of your marketing effort is wasted. The typical prospect will need to hear from you (or about you) 5-7 times before deciding to work with you. And most marketing approaches need a follow-through element to succeed. For example, attending networking events requires post-event follow-up with the people you meet. Online networking requires regular participation, not just posting when you have something to promote.

5. MARKETING APPROACH: Are the strategies and tactics you are using to reach your market the most effective approaches available to you? Are they appropriate for your target market, and a good match for your skills and personality?

Only after addressing the first four problem areas above should you think about changing *how* you market. Because in truth, your tactics may not need to change. Whether you've been marketing yourself with cold calling, public speaking, or social networking, once you are spending enough time, marketing to the right people, delivering a targeted message, and following through on all your efforts, your results will improve dramatically.

So finding new or different marketing approaches—the place where most people *start* to fix their marketing—is actually the last area to consider. The most effective approaches are those that include personal contact with your prospects, increase your credibility, and lend themselves to building relationships over time. And, approaches that match your skills and personality are more likely to succeed because you will actually use them instead of resisting them.

Once you know what might be stopping your marketing from being successful, make a commitment to fix what's really wrong. Resist the temptation (and hype) to keep trying new "silver bullet" marketing tactics or overloading yourself with endless possibilities. Finding the right answers will be much easier when you're trying to solve the right problem.

C.J. Hayden, MCC, CPCC, is the bestselling author of *Get Clients Now!, The One-Person Marketing Plan Workbook,* and over 400 articles. C.J. is a business coach and teacher who helps entrepreneurs get clients, get strategic, and get things done. Her company, Wings for Business, specializes in serving self-employed professionals and solopreneurs.

A popular speaker and workshop leader, C.J. has presented hundreds of programs on marketing and entrepreneurship to corporate clients, professional associations, and small businesses. She has taught marketing for John F. Kennedy University, Mills College, the U.S. Small Business Administration, and SCORE. She contributes regularly to dozens of magazines and websites,

including Home Business, RainToday, and About.com.
www.getclientsnow.com
info@getclientsnow.com   (877) 946-4722

Book Two:
Get More Referrals

How to Take Your Great First Impression to the Next Level:

Get More Referrals

Debra started her day telling herself, "Get referrals today. Get referrals today!" She met with three clients. During each meeting, she remembered to get referrals. But each time, she said to herself, "No. This is not the time. I mean this customer might have second thoughts. I do not want to gum up this sale." The result: Debra failed to ask for referrals in all three situations.

Have you had similar experiences? I have. What causes us to fail to ask for referrals?

- First, we may not know how.
- Second, we may feel that we're imposing on the person.
- Third, the specter for rejection looms over us, promising pain.

Fortunately, I have studied with mentors to learn how to smoothly ask for referrals in a way that the customer, or even a relative stranger feels comfortable in connecting me with others.

Along the way, I have innovated some methods.

We'll use the G.A.I.N.S. process.

G – Get the words out
A – Ask at the best time
I – Initiate giving
N – Nurture trust
S – Seed the "referrals" idea

1. Get the words out

I have found that getting the words out can be tough! So I have devised ways to just get started.

I'll begin with one of these phrases:

- I'm curious...
- I'm wondering...
- Oh, I have a question for you...

Then, I add something like:

- Who do you know who wants to...?
- Who do you know, perhaps, a co-worker or someone you met recently at an industry event, who said that they...?

When I say, "Who do you know?" I'm getting my brain to shift into finding something specific to help the other person find a certain memory so they can discover someone who may be a lead for me.

The point is: Many times, when salespeople ask for a referral, the other person has no way of accessing their memories of anyone they know who may be in the market for a particular product or service.

Imagine that a person's memory is a file cabinet. You need to give the listener a clue that functions like a handle on a particular drawer of that memory-file cabinet.

That's the reason that it is helpful to say something like:

- Who do you know, perhaps, you were talking with a friend recently, who said, "Oh, I've got to get organized"?
- Who do you know, perhaps, your team leader who said, we must streamline the XYZ process...?"

2. Ask at the best time

The best time to ask for a referral is immediately after the sales transaction is complete. As soon as the person signs the approval paperwork for your product, they're in a good mood. At this moment, they love you the best, they love the product the best, and they feel the best. Researchers show that people get a rush of endorphins after they make a decision. So jump at this opportunity-moment. Ask for a referral.

The second best time is any time when you feel that the person "knows you, likes you, and trusts you." (This phrase is from author Bob Burg.)

3. Initiate giving

There is a universal law that you give first and then receive. Plant a seed, nurture it, infuse the soil with nutrients, and the soil will give you corn or a flower.

Give the person something that shows you *know* what you're talking about. A video, a booklet, or a special report you wrote—all of these things accomplish two objectives. First, you demonstrate your credibility. Second, you create a desire for the other person to reciprocate, that is, make the "score" even between you two. Subconsciously, people dislike having a pending debt. So they do something in return to alleviate that subconscious discomfort. It is reported that a lot of sales were initiated simply because a salesperson gave someone a pen.

As a side note: one thing I do to support budding authors is invite someone to request my article: "How You Can Take Suffering Out of Writing"—which is an excerpt from my book, *Love Yourself to Financial Abundance and Spiritual Joy.*

Further, I offer at my blog BeHeardandBeTrusted.com, the free report "9 Deadly Mistakes to Avoid for Your Next

Speech and 9 Surefire Ways to Speak Well."

It is easier for me to get referrals when someone experiences the value I provide. A number of people at Facebook have shared my video "How You Can Believe in Yourself Even When Others Don't." You can access this seven minute video on YouTube by typing "Believe in Yourself Tom Marcoux" into the search box.

4. Nurture trust

Throughout this book, a major theme arises often: Be trustworthy. Earlier I mentioned that listening well helps the other person trust you.

Here I want to emphasize that you need to avoid "Trust-breakers" that include: a) arriving late for a meeting, b) not fulfilling a promise to provide information when you said you would, and c) being slow to return phone calls and emails.

Instead, nurture trust by living up to T.H.O.R.—trustworthy, helpful, organized and respectful.

5. Seed the "referrals" idea

To get more referrals it really helps to plant the seed of the "referrals" idea.

Here is an example. In some of my presentations (when appropriate), I plant the seed of how attendees can benefit from working with me as their personal coach. You will notice that I make the whole demonstration relevant to the audience.

Tom: "So today, I'll share with you how to get referrals. You see I primarily work on a referral basis. For example, I'm a personal coach. Who would like to work with me now? I'll do some personal coaching with you now. [Soon I'm seated on the stage with a volunteer.]

Tom: So you're Ginny — yes?

Ginny: Yes.

Tom: What would you like to work on?

Ginny: A lot of things.

[Ginny, audience and Tom chuckle.]

Tom: I'm right there with you. I've worked with coaches on a number of topics. And, today, this moment, what do you want to work on?

Ginny: Eating better.

Tom: Sounds good. And what does eating better mean to you?

Ginny: More fruits, more vegetables. Less processed snacks. I tend to eat some sugary breakfast bar in the morning.

Tom: So, specifically, you want to eat better in the morning and you want to eat better snacks?

Ginny: Yes.

Tom: Good. So in my form of coaching we focus on four things. [Tom writes on board. G.A.I.N.]

- Get to the Heart of It
- Acquire New Knowledge
- Intensify Systems
- Nurture New Results

Tom: When you eat better in the morning and you eat better snacks what do you get?

Ginny: Uh – healthy.

Tom: When you have that — how will you feel?

Ginny: Well...better.

Tom: You'll have more energy?

Ginny: Yes. And well, I'll probably lose some weight.

Tom: So feeling more energy and dropping some weight are important you?

Ginny: Yes.

Tom: What's most important to you?

Ginny: Feeling more energy.

Tom: So you see, when you Get to the Heart of It. You want to feel—

Ginny: More energy.

Tom (gives her a pen and paper): When you write these next things down, you'll have your own Action Plan because you want New Results. An Action Plan really works when you place in new Systems.

In fact, a habit is defined as a conditioned response. We form habits through a pattern or a system of behaviors. It all starts with a trigger. So we're going to use the Trigger Set Method.

[At this point, Tom helps Ginny develop her own system to eat better and increase her personal energy. The work is personalized to Ginny's preferences and personal ways of being in the world. Near the end of the discussion, Tom includes the following . . .]

Tom: As you know, I work on referrals. So after this, Ginny, you can tell people and you learned about the—

Ginny (and audience members): Trigger Set Method

Tom: Well done! Well done, everybody. (Tom smiles.) When people give me referrals for coaching, they mention about the 4 Elements of Coaching that I do. It's all about G.A.I.N. [Tom points to the words on the board.]

Get to the Heart of It

Acquire New Knowledge

Intensify Systems

Nurture New Results.

Tom: So Ginny, you're going to—

Ginny: Combine activities. I'll enjoy listening to music while I pre-setup my snacks in the refrigerator.

Tom: And about the Trigger Set Method. Your trigger is—

Ginny: Seeing the refrigerator. So I'll immediately open the refrigerator, open a baggie and pop an orange slice in my mouth.

Tom (big smile): Sounds great! And now, Ginny you've had a brief coaching session with me. And this worked for you?

Ginny (smiling): Yes?

Tom: Great. Since I work on referrals, I'm wondering, who do you know, maybe someone you work with or someone you met at a workshop, who can benefit from working with me?

[Ginny turns to the audience; she looks at a friend]

Ginny: Well, there's Sarah.

Tom: (pulls out five 3x5 cards): That's terrific. I look forward to talking with you, Sarah. (Tom writes Sarah's name on one of the 5 cards). And next—

(addresses the audience) Let's all give Ginny a round of applause. We've learned so much from Ginny. For example, she outs her friend, Sarah—

(Ginny and audience laugh).

Thank you, Ginny.

[Ginny returns to her seat.]

Tom (turns to audience): So we learned a number of things. Remember, we're talking about planting seeds of the "give me referrals" idea.

For the coaching session, you know that I work on—

Audience: Referrals.

Tom: So who can give me referrals?
Audience: Ginny.
Tom: And all of you. You saw how I do personal coaching.

In the above example, I planted the seed of "I work on referral" multiple times. And research shows that to inspire someone to new action we need to connect with them, often about five times. By planting the seed, "I work on referral," and connecting them to my expertise through demonstrating my skills as a personal coach, I am increasing my chances of receiving my desired outcome: getting more business.

A "Clever" Way for Getting Referrals

One of my Facebook friends asked about running a contest to serve people and to get them interested in what she offers. I replied:

"Susan, it depends on what you do and how you want to serve more people. For example, if you were an author, you could have people write a paragraph about their difficulty. Let's say you were a time management expert, you could have people write a paragraph about their time management problem and their unusual solution. The winning stories could end up in your next book and you could give ebook copies to the winners. [You can adapt this pattern in some way . . . possibly.] The whole idea is to make the contest relevant to the theme of what you do when you work with people."

An Important Method for Getting More Referrals

I call this "Aim for 5." One effective dentist pulls out five 3x5 cards and asks for five referrals. He does this after he has heard the patient say something good about his work. The dentist says: "As you know, I work on referrals. That's why I'm able to devote more attention and time to great patients like you. So who do you know who...?"

It's rare that someone will give five referrals. Usually they come through with three referrals (and that's better than one!).

The above "get referrals methods" require rehearsal. You will need to try them in the real world and adjust them to your own, personal ways of talking.

You will be proud of yourself and happy about your better results once you go into action and get more referrals.

* * *

How to Take Your Great First Impression to the Next Level:

Become Strong and Overcome Rejection

A number of salespeople fail to ask for a referral because they feel, deep down, a fear of rejection. This means so much to me that I wrote the below article for my blog at www.BeHeardandBeTrusted.com on the topic of rejection in general:

As his horse spun around, my father held on, captive on a runaway horse.

He had to duck his head as the horse raced into the barn. Otherwise, he would have left a "face print" on the barn door frame. This horse *rejected* the idea that this afternoon was about walking on the beach. Horses, other beings and people are likely to give us some resistance and even some outright rejection. We will use the C.A.N. process for dealing with rejection. Use these methods and become strong:

C – cancel the "3 Deadly Perceptions"

A – align with "what works" and "areas to improve"

N – nurture your "let go ritual" and "go forward ritual"

1. Cancel the "3 Deadly Perceptions"

Do you know someone who shoots down every new idea with comments like: "That won't work. I tried that already. It didn't work."

It's likely that this person suffers from a point of view dominated by the *3 Deadly Perceptions*. It is the viewpoint that something bad is Personal, Pervasive, and Permanent.

It sounds like this: "No. I didn't get the job offer. There's something wrong with me *[personal]*. In fact, I always screw up job interviews *[pervasive]*. I'll never get better at this *[permanent]*."

The above disempowering habit of thinking can keep a person stuck in an unhealthy cycle.

It's often *not* even true!

For example, imagine a kid saying, "I fell off the bicycle when learning how to ride for the first time. I always fall off. I'll never learn to ride a bicycle ever."

With some key words of coaching, this kid can learn to ride a bike!

The solution is to *Turn Around the Words*.

Personal	*Not personal*
I always screw up job interviews.	We did not have a match.
Pervasive	*Not pervasive*
I mess up every interview.	This was just one interview. I've learned something; I'll do better on the next interview.

Permanent	Not permanent
I won't find a job.	We did not have a match. I'll find a job and company that are a good fit for me. And they'll like the great job I do for the team.

In a sense, my opening story of my father and the errant horse relates to this point. It is NOT pervasive and permanent if you *"get on another horse!"*

That was the solution for my father that day. The stable team found another horse, one that was *cooperative,* and my father and I enjoyed riding horses down the beach in Half Moon Bay, California.

Now it's your turn.

Do you have a "reflex" to use words that program you in a negative direction? — that is, do you say things that hold to something bad as personal, pervasive, and permanent?

How can you turn your words into an empowering direction?

2. Align with "what works" and "areas to improve"

When I went on auditions for film and commercials, I used a journal. For every audition, I wrote *"what works"* (for example, "I mentioned my martial arts experience") and *"areas to improve"* (for example, "Next time, I'll make sure to show a whole range of that southern accent.")

After I wrote down my encouraging words "what works" and the lessons learned "areas to improve" — I closed the journal. (I called this my *What Works/Areas to Improve Journal.*)

This was *an improvement* over the torture of ruminating

that fellow actors and I regularly fell into.

Make any rejection situation transform into another experience when you learn and get stronger.

3. Nurture your "Let Go Ritual" and "Go Forward Ritual"

Years ago, the top time management/day planner company flew me into Utah. I stayed in a great hotel and had a good dinner at their expense. The next day I auditioned alongside two other finalists to be one of their time management strategy presenters.

Later, I flew home and was soon informed that I did not get the job. It hurt badly. (I think that one of the other finalists, the attractive, articulate blond young woman, got the job.)

I felt rejected and hugely disappointed. But I did NOT stay there. Immediately, I implemented a "Go Forward Ritual." In this case, my *Go Forward* actions were to rent a space and give a time management workshop built on my OWN material.

I did not have to wait for someone else to say *yes* to me. I stepped forward on my own.

This process echoed the time when my high school best friend replaced me as the leader of the movie production club that I had founded. I did not stay in the "the upperclassmen rejected me" place of thinking. Instead, my *Go Forward actions* were to start a new production club—the TV production club. Nothing would stop me from leading a team of students to make video productions. [This means so much to me that I wrote a book *Nothing Can Stop You This Year!*]

I have taken many appropriate risks. Sometimes, I've been rejected. I implement two things: a **"Let Go Ritual"** and **"Go Forward Ritual."**

But this was not the only thing I had to do because I also learned that letting go of the disappointment, anger, resentment, sadness, and rejection helps you heal and stay happy and productive. So I also developed a "Let Go Ritual."

In recent years, my Let Go Ritual is *"Celebrate Someone Disagrees."*

If someone rejects you as a friend, rejects what you're selling or something else . . . they are disagreeing. The person does not agree with you about the value of something.

So what do you celebrate? **You celebrate your efforts and your courage to reach out to people. You celebrate that you're taking steps forward.**

Some of my clients celebrate by getting together with a friend or even buying an empowering song from iTunes.

Here's another form of a Let Go Ritual: Have a sheet of paper with "No" inscribed 20 times. At the bottom of the sheet inscribe "YES!" Every time you hear "no," cross off a "No" on the paper. Now, you are one step closer to a *golden Yes!*

One salesperson has this Go Forward Ritual: If a sales phone call results in a rejection, the person places a quarter in a bowl and says out loud (after the call), "Next!" Then she places a smile on her face and makes the next phone call.

* * *

Put some attention and effort into making sure your daily actions strengthen you.

Be sure to develop your habit of writing in a *What Works/Areas to Improve Journal.* Instill some Let Go Rituals and Go Forward Rituals.

Successful people face more rejection than "average" people. Why? Successful people take more risks and with that, they can lose at times. We just hear about their successes.

Author Zig Ziglar said, "No one would go bowling if they couldn't see the pins drop."

I'll add: "No one would go bowling if the pins automatically dropped and there was no challenge."

Author Will Bowen wrote: "Problems keep us engaged."

I'll add: "Problems, including rejection, keep us growing, moving forward and having an interesting, fulfilling life."

Go forward.

* * *

To get referrals, be sure to put yourself in the right place at the right time. You need to make good decisions including which networking event to attend because you have to be selective. Now we will cover a strategy for making great decisions:

Expand Your Success: Secrets so You Make Great Decisions!

"Teach another class or start a home-based business," my client Donna was stumped, trying to make a good decision. Do you worry a lot when confronted with tough decisions? I will now share methods I use for making good decisions. We will use the W.I.N. process:

W – Wonder and answer questions
I – Intensify your focus
N – Notice what you say

1. Wonder and answer questions

To get new and better results, we do well by asking questions and discovering a new approach to situations that arise. When you face a tough decision, ask yourself these questions:

1. What can I gain?
2. Is this gain aligned with my long-term goals?
3. What do I lose if I do not take advantage of this opportunity?
4. What could go wrong? How bad might the damage be? (Can I fix it?)
5. What is the opportunity cost*?

* *The New Oxford American Dictionary* defines an *opportunity cost* as "the loss of potential gain from other alternatives when one alternative is chosen."

Another way to say this is: You will lose something when you say *yes* to one alternative. There is a cost—a price.

You can ask yourself this question: "When I say *yes* to this, what do I lose by saying *no* to something else?"

Make sure that when you say *yes*, you are heading in the direction of **what you really want**.

It really helps to "think on paper." Write down your thoughts, questions and answers on paper and your problem looks smaller and more manageable. You'll also see new connections between the details you have written on paper.

2. Intensify your focus

Many people I've met are focused on complaining. Instead, *intensify your focus* on possible good that may result from your decision.

A few authors suggest that if something is "not a Hell Yes! then it is a 'Hell No!'" These authors emphasize that you would do well in clearing your life of things you feel lukewarm about—as much as possible.

For example, my most important focus point is my series of graphic novels called *Jack AngelSword*. So I work on this project everyday. It is a Hell Yes! for me.

Another way to intensify your focus relates to my phrase: **"Success is the intersection of what you're Good At with what people will Pay For and which Clients You Want."**

It may take time and some experimenting to find out what is a great fit for you.

Now it's your turn. Ask yourself:
- What am I good at?
- Who will pay for it?
- Are these people the clients that I want?

3. Notice what you say

When you ask friends for opinions, do *not* only listen for their insights. **Listen to what YOU say.** Notice how YOU feel as you express your thoughts and feelings about alternatives when you are aiming to make a decision.

About Using Two Lists of "Pro" and "Con"

Some people think that if you have more "Pro" reasons to do something then, by the numbers, you should take that action.

I've learned that your intuition will help you if you "feel your way through" the process of looking at both the pro and the con.

For example, one year I was deciding about taking a particular position at a bank.

I had 9 reasons to take the position.

However, when I wrote down the "con" reasons, I stopped at the third reason to refuse the job offer. That *3rd Reason Against the Job Offer* essentially jumped off the page in my feelings.

Later, my sweetheart described the situation as: "Your reason to refuse the job offer was a *watermelon* while the 'pro' reasons were just *raisins.*"

Now it's your turn.

Write down your reasons for and against taking action. Then let your intuition alert you to what is a "watermelon" (strong reason) or a raisin (inconsequential reason).

Developing your decision-making skills is vital for doubling your success.

Decision-making is easy if your values are clear." – Roy O. Disney (partner and brother of Walt Disney)

Make good decisions and enjoy better results.

The best to you on your path.

Tom Marcoux

Book Three:
Do Something Better Than
Standard Follow Up

Do You Know the Secret Behind Great Success? (Secrets of Great Follow Up)

Some years ago, I had business cards from nine people after first meeting them at a Chamber of Commerce event.

I knew I should follow up with them. But then I hesitated. I had some disempowering feelings like: "Oh, they'll think I'm bothering them" and "They'll think I'm trying to sell them something."

Did I follow up? No. In fact, their business cards got lost in a file somewhere.

Can you relate to that experience?

Years later, I have learned how to be more skillful about new contacts and follow-up.

Do you want to truly expand your success? Learn to transform how you follow up with people. Many people simply fail to follow up because of two incomplete perceptions that follow up is "drudgery" and "bothering someone again." Stop! You can make follow up into something that the other person welcomes—and that you're comfortable doing! You will actually feel good as you do the follow up activities.

First you need to transform "follow up" into what I call "Follow-Good." The other person feels good while you contact them, and you feel good about the process. You stop dreading your follow-up actions. We will use the G.O.O.D. process:

G – Get ready ahead of time
O – Organize a system
O – Open dialogue
D – Do follow up in 2 minute segments

1. Get ready ahead of time
The essence of "Follow-Good" is to transform yourself from an intruder into a "host" and an "invited guest."

To do this, you need to get ready ahead of time.

For example, when I attend an in-person networking event, I bring 3x5 cards. Why? So I can take notes at an appropriate time. For example, if you are talking with someone from an Asian culture do NOT write on their business card. I hold my 3x5 card next to their card and I write notes on the 3x5 card and then place the person's card into my folded 3x5 card. Then the cards are together, and they go into my pre-selected pocket.

The above process is for you to identify what the person is interested in. This will give you clues as to what you can give to the person in order to brighten his or her life. Let's say that Sarah's daughter is taking karate classes, you can send a copy of an article that shows how girls can excel in martial art classes.

Bob Burg, author of *Endless Referrals*, emphasizes the value of sending people a hand-written follow-up card. Here is how you can get ready ahead of time.

In advance, set up your thank you cards. Have them ready to go in a #10 envelope, with your handwritten return address, and hand-applied postage stamp.

Then, the same night of a networking event, fill out the cards (which have your photo and contact information) and place the completed cards in a mailbox. [Sure, you could send an email message, but everybody does that—no one stands out.]

2. Organize a system

To do follow up effectively and with little pain, it is good to use a system. As you develop this system, think of ways for you to streamline the system into easy steps. *You need to feel good* as YOU do the follow-up work. Hence my phrase: "Follow-Good." You are actually doing a good work. You're providing a benefit for the other person.

Here is an example of a system:

1) Meet the person at a networking event.

2) Send an email the same night of the first encounter OR send a follow-up, handwritten card (in a #10 envelope).

3) Place in your calendar system a prompt to remind you to find a suitable article that might be useful to the person.

4) Print out that article and send it.

Each person will find how to customize his or her own system. Bob Burg suggests that one send a notepad with one's photo and contact information on each page.

Bob feels that such a notepad keeps you in front of the prospective client's face.

3. Open dialogue

Consider your follow up activities as continuing a positive dialogue with the new person. And certainly, connect with the person simply to say, "How are things going?" This works well in social media. Often, I will see that someone is online and available for a chat at Facebook. So I simply type, "Andrea, how are things going?" Then I "listen" as they often vent about something. With me, they have an empathetic ear. The person sees that I am demonstrating care and concern.

4. Do follow up in two minute segments

What gets done? Something that is easy and fast to do. You can follow up with a person in a short amount of time. For example, in 1988 a *New York Times* article revealed how movie mogul Jeffrey Katzenberg made up 600 phone calls a week. He was called "the master of the two minute phone call." Katzenberg had two secretaries who split the Katzenberg day between them. They placed the calls and had people hold on so that Katzenberg could go from one conversation to the next.

Katzenberg's example is extreme. But we can take some inspiration that it is valuable to stay in contact with people.

Here is another example. Consider having an open file carton next to your desk. When you think of a follow-up idea, jot it down and toss it into the open file for a particular person.

(You can also jot the idea down in a reminder that you place into an online calendar system.)

A really powerful *Follow-Good* practice is to jot a handwritten note down in two minutes. Later, in the day, take two minutes and get that note into the mail.

Praise people. Celebrate their day.

A while ago, I called a friend and said, "Happy today. We can celebrate that one year ago today, you finished writing your first book!"

People appreciate that you notice their special days.

Use these "Follow-Good" methods:

G – Get ready ahead of time

O – Organize a system

O – Open dialogue

D – Do follow up in 2 minute segments

Consider asking people in your networking circle these

important questions:

- How can I recognize a good client for you?
- How can I be supportive of what you're doing?

When they tell you, you can get some time to consider how you might help. (I call such time "thinkspace.")

You could reply with something like: "I hear you. It would be great for me to promote your book from my Facebook wall. I need to double-check a couple of things. How about I get back to you on Thursday afternoon?"

One of my clients faced such a situation. When she got back to the person, she said, "I've found a way to be helpful. I can send out a tweet about your new book. I'm comfortable with that."

Remember, we can develop a Circle of Success.

We can actually feel good about how we help other people. We become the "host" of good things that we do—including connecting people in our network.

When you call, you will be treated like an invited guest.

This is all based on what I call "The Three Magic Words of Networking: 'Help Them First.'"

Good journey.

* * *

Now, we will learn excellent follow up methods from C.J. Hayden.

44 Ways to Follow Up with Your Prospects
by C.J. Hayden, MCC, CPCC

You know you need to follow up with prospective clients, but you often find yourself putting it off. "I already called them three times," you think. Or, "They never answer the phone anyway." Or, "I hate hearing no." Or, "I don't want to bug them." Or, "What do I say that's new?"

It's only natural to resist placing phone calls to prospects who didn't return your last call, never seem to be there, may not be ready to buy, or might say they're not interested. But here's the good news. Calling prospects on the phone and asking them to hire you is not the only way to follow up!

Yes, you can call your prospects on the phone, but you can also email them, send a letter or note by postal mail, fax them, overnight them a package, send a text message, or instant message them online. And those are just the different communication channels you might use. The type of messages you deliver can be much more varied than simply asking prospects to do business.

Consider the following 44 ways that you can follow up with your prospects via any communication channel you choose, in order to build a relationship, remind them of what you do, and present yourself as a valuable resource and expert in your field. Many of these follow-up approaches can also be used with potential referral sources and networking contacts.

1. Ask if they have new questions about what you last discussed.
2. Tell them about a book, article, video, or website that might help with what you talked about.
3. Send a personal note with a copy of your brochure or fact sheet.
4. Point them to a vendor who can solve one of their issues you don't address.
5. Prepare a personalized marketing kit for them focused on their unique issues.
6. Tell them about an upcoming event that addresses an issue you think they have.

7. Invite them to an event where you are a speaker, organizer, or sponsor.
8. Attend an event where you are likely to run into them.
9. Send a nice-to-meet-you or good-to-see-you note with your business card.
10. Call or email to ask what's new in their world.
11. Leave a brief benefits-oriented commercial on their voice mail.
12. Ask them to meet you for coffee, a drink, or lunch.
13. Invite them for golf, tennis, a bike ride, or a walk in the park.
14. Invite them to a concert, play, reading, or art opening.
15. Offer to stop by their place of business.
16. Send a letter summarizing what you last talked about and suggesting next steps.
17. Ask for a meeting so you can prepare a detailed proposal for them.
18. Send them an article (or link to one) that you have written.
19. Send them an article someone else has written about a topic relevant to them.
20. Send them a present — chocolate, cookies, flowers, a plant, a bottle of wine, or a book.
21. Send them a birthday card.
22. Send them a joke or cartoon about their industry or your field.
23. Send a postcard reminding them what you do.
24. Tell them about a special offer available if they act now.
25. Offer them a free sample of what you can do for them.

26. Send an announcement about a new development in your business.
27. Send a copy of your newsletter or post from your blog and invite them to subscribe.
28. Send a link to a print, audio, or video interview with you about your work.
29. Send a link to a video where you share helpful tips or a client success story.
30. Refer them a prospect for their own business.
31. Watch for their posts on Facebook, Twitter, LinkedIn, or Google + and comment on them.
32. Post something useful to an online community where they are members.
33. Post a comment on their blog.
34. Invite them to visit your updated website.
35. Make them a free offer that will subscribe them to an autoresponder series.
36. Give a free teleclass or webinar and invite all your prospects.
37. Invite them to an open house, reception, demonstration, or free workshop.
38. Host a networking breakfast or brown bag lunch and invite several prospects.
39. Offer to give a talk or brown bag lunch for their organization at no charge.
40. Write a white paper or case study and send it to all your prospects.
41. Ask the person who introduced you to contact them and mention you again.
42. Introduce them to a colleague of yours they might like to know.
43. Volunteer for an organization where they also serve.

44. And of course, you can always ask if they are ready to start working with you.

Following up consistently is one of the most productive marketing activities there is, but it won't work if you don't do it. The next time you realize you are avoiding follow-up, pull out your prospect list and choose an approach at random from the suggestions above. It matters much less how you follow up than it does that you follow up.

C.J. Hayden, MCC, CPCC, is the bestselling author of *Get Clients Now!, The One-Person Marketing Plan Workbook,* and over 400 articles. C.J. is a business coach and teacher who helps entrepreneurs get clients, get strategic, and get things done. Her company, Wings for Business, specializes in serving self-employed professionals and solopreneurs.

A popular speaker and workshop leader, C.J. has presented hundreds of programs on marketing and entrepreneurship to corporate clients, professional associations, and small businesses. She has taught marketing for John F. Kennedy University, Mills College, the U.S. Small Business Administration, and SCORE. She contributes regularly to dozens of magazines and websites, including Home Business, RainToday, and About.com.

www.getclientsnow.com

info@getclientsnow.com   (877) 946-4722

* * *

When you do excellent follow-up or what I call "Follow Good," you can even ask for a favor in a graceful and effective manner.

Effectively Asking for a Favor and Power Networking

Anne couldn't believe it: a guy she had not seen since high school finds her on Facebook and then immediately asks her to use her employee discount to help him get a low priced couch.

"How rude!" Anne told her friend Merla. "And how stupid," Anne concluded.

Similarly, I have seen it happen when some people who are generally kind and friendly, blurt out a request. It is almost as if they do not thrust themselves to wait an appropriate time and build a friendship.

A similar thing happens when someone makes a rash decision. The tension of not deciding hurts too much so the person makes a decision—any decision.

But this is NOT for you.

In this section we will talk about how to effectively ask for a favor.

First, avoid these two significant mistakes:

- Avoid asking immediately
- Avoid reminding and reducing the interaction to "a trade"

Some years ago, I made the "reminding" mistake. For my friend Sam, I provided some typing and I said, "Well, since I did some typing for you, how about you help me sorting some receipts?" I saw a frown hit Sam's face, and I heard in his tone when he begrudgingly said, "Hrph. All right." His face told the story that he felt cornered.

There *is* a better approach.

Jodi Glickman in her article "Asking for a Favor: The Three Keys" [https://hbr.org/2011/01/asking-for-a-favor-the] noted three keys:

- Set the Stage: "I have a favor to ask you"
- Give a Reason [Use "because"]
- Provide an Escape Clause

Now, I'll express some ideas about the Three Keys noted above:

1) Set the Stage: "I have a favor to ask you"

People do not like to be blindsided. When you say, "I have a favor to ask you," in a sense, you are giving them some warning. They will pause and likely hear you out.

2) Give a Reason [use "because"]

When you express a reason, you open the door that the other person may be able to relate to your situation. Also, to be clear, no one wants to be taken for granted. So it causes trouble to assume that someone will "just jump" when you make a request.

However, when you provide a good reason, the person feels respected.

You could say something like: "I know you're busy. I'm only asking at this time *because* if I don't clear the apartment and make sure it's in good shape, I'll lose the security deposit."

Further, psychologist Ellen Langer conducted research and found that the word "because" was all that was needed to get more people to allow someone to cut in line when a number of people were waiting to use one copier.

"Because" made the difference to the tune of 93% compliance instead of a mere 60% when people did not hear "because." That is a 33% difference!

What reason did the researcher provide?—"because I need to make copies." It appears that the word "because" is a powerful word!

3) Provide an Escape Clause

Earlier, I mentioned my "reminding" mistake and how my friend Sam felt cornered. Avoid pushing people. Instead, show your understanding and give the person the space to refuse your request. You could say something like: "I know you're busy. I'm only asking at this time *because* if I don't clear the apartment and make sure it's in good shape, I'll lose the security deposit. Still, I realize that you've been under extra pressure lately. So if this won't work for you I understand. I'll figure something out."

Be sure to make your tone light. A vocal tone is often stronger than the words you use. Make sure that "how you say it" really provides the Escape Clause.

A cornered person will likely feel resentment. At that point, they will likely "push back." Avoid that!

Provide the Escape Clause.

A Special Note: Rehearse how you will say your request. Since your vocal tone is crucial, practice keeping your tone light and avoid pushing.

The point is: asking for a favor, receiving help and returning a favor all work best when they seem natural and not forced.

Further, if you do not rehearse and you do not ask for favors in an appropriate manner, you are really losing an important part of the value in having a networking circle. In other words, you fail to accomplish Power Networking.

Instead, realize: **People often feel good when they help someone.** It is fine for you to ask for help. It creates good will. In fact, research shows that people feel closer to someone they have helped.

So create good relationships by making appropriate requests in a savvy manner. Be sure to also return favors. In fact, use the principle I mention elsewhere in this book: The Three Magic Words of Networking: *Help Them First.*

Tom Marcoux

Book Four:
Create a Great Personal Brand and Enhance Your Power Networking

Create Your Personal Brand and Power Networking

Frank closed his speech and received thunderous applause. As he stood at his autograph table that featured his book, a woman walked up and said, "Frank you, brought important points. I think I could use some coaching."

As my client, Frank recounted his feeling at that point: "Wow! How easy. I just give a speech and the group looks on me as an expert. My personal brand is so much stronger and attractive. I got two clients immediately."

To have people in your networking circle poised to help you, it helps for them to have the answer to two questions:

- Who is your ideal client and how can I recognize them?
- What is your *personal brand*?

Your *personal brand* is, in essence, two things: a) your promise of performance and b) your answer to the question "What are you best known for?"

We'll use the B.R.A.N.D. process to build your personal brand so that you can increase your success.

B – Build your "best known" answer

R – Respect the promise

A – Ask "what's most important to you"

N – Nurture "T.H.O.R."

D – Devote efforts to the "Success Triangle"

1. Build your "best known" answer

As I mentioned, the essence of your personal brand is your answer to the question "What are you best known for?" You already have a personal brand. The important question is do you like your personal brand and is it serving your highest good?

For example, I have a friend who has not been on time for any social event in seven years. Then he shocked me and said, "Tom, I want to work with you." I did *not* hire this person, and the reason is that I cannot trust him. His personal brand is "unreliable and disrespectful of other people's time."

Instead, decide what *positive* attributes you want people to think of when your name arises in conversation. What five words do you want people to think of when you're mentioned in a conversation?

My clients have described the words they want applied to them: "Reliable, knowledgeable, on-time, top provider of _____."

For example, my team has developed a moniker for me: Tom Marcoux, Spoken Word Strategist. This implies that I can help people excel in speeches, team meetings and sales presentations.

Now it's your turn.

Write down in your journal, the ideal answer to "What are you best known for?"

2. Respect the promise

Your personal brand is a promise of performance. At one time, Tony Robbins used the moniker "America's Results Coach." So the promise is that Tony will help his client gain results. Build your actions around delivering on your promise of performance. Make sure that you can come through. For example, years ago, I was on a television show. The host said, "How do people find you? What is your website?" I replied, "TomMarcoux.com." He asked, "How do you spell Marcoux?" I knew I was in trouble then.

So I went to my team and we came up with TomSuperCoach.com

I knew that people in my industry would tease me, and I received emails addressed, "Hi Super Tom." Still, I study every day and I coach people every week. So I am certain I can deliver on the promise of providing excellent coaching.

3. Ask "what's most important to you"

Ask your clients and prospective clients: "What's most important to you about [my product/service]?"

Doing so helps you discover what your clients' biggest concerns are and how your product solves their problems. Build your personal brand around being a *problem solver* for your clientele's greatest needs.

Over the years, I have observed what my readers and clients want. Also I have observed what my audiences respond to the most. This led me to refine my message into: "Success is Charisma, Confidence and Consistent Action." I refer to the "3 C's of Success."

Now it's your turn.

What questions about what you offer (product/service) will you ask your clients about? How will you discover what is most important to them?

4. Nurture "T.H.O.R."

Earlier, I mentioned how one of my friends has the personal brand (among his friends) of being unreliable and disrespectful. This led me to include "respectful" as a prime element of an excellent personal brand. For my clients, I made this mnemonic device of T.H.O.R. which includes: Trustworthy, Helpful, Organized and Respectful.

Be sure that your actions and your stories reflect how you have all of the T.H.O.R. elements of a great personal brand. Be careful to avoid telling stories about how you made errors in which you seem disorganized. Such stories would undermine your excellent personal brand.

Instead, talk about how clients have found you to be truly helpful, organized and trustworthy.

Write in your journal examples/stories of how you have been Trustworthy, Helpful, Organized and Respectful.

5. Devote efforts to the "Success Triangle"

To build your powerful personal brand, it really helps to focus on which clients you really want to work with. For example, one author said that she posted on her website: "no whiners, complainers or chronic cynics." Many of her colleagues celebrated her courage to have people "weed themselves out" so only those who are really ready to work will call upon her.

I have created a shorthand way to refer to how to organize your business and efforts for your own best morale and productivity. I call this the *Success Triangle*. My phrase is: "Success arises from what you're *Good At*, what people will *Pay For*, and what *Clients You Want*."

Orchestrate your personal brand so that you attract the Clients You Want—those who want to Pay For what you are Good At. Not only will you enjoy your workdays, you will attract more and more business. As a result, your personal brand will be golden.

* * *

A great personal brand conveys your confidence in your well-earned skills.

How You Can Make an Impression as a Confident Person (Confident Not Arrogant)

"I hate that guy," Gil said to his friend, Jonathan.

Gil continued, "Nathan thinks he knows everything."

Jonathan protested, "No. Nathan just appears like that. I've been around him when he's admitted mistakes. He doesn't take himself too seriously."

The confusion about whether Nathan is confident and not arrogant is an example of a number of ways impressions can get mixed up.

Here are three particular situations:

1) Confident not arrogant
2) Approachable not aloof
3) Helpful not a doormat

1) Confident not arrogant

A confident person does *not* need to dominate a conversation.

A confident person would say something like: "I think XY needs to happen, and here are my reasons." On the other hand, an arrogant person would say, "Those 1-2-3 guys haven't got a clue. I know the right thing—it's the only thing to do in this situation."

Further, an arrogant person, while dominating a conversation, dumps all of his or her accomplishments on the listener. It is similar to hearing someone recite their resume.

The solution is to only "**sprinkle**" an admirable detail or two.

For example, you might say, "I'm looking forward to returning to the recording studio to begin producing my new song." Then say a related question to the other person like: "What's one of your favorite songs or works of music?"

With the question, you turn the spotlight of the conversation back onto the other person.

2) Approachable not aloof

Some years ago, I was walking with my father through the neighborhood where he lives. He has certain people in the neighborhood with whom he stops and has a conversation.

I had been working several days in a row and I was tired. I was not up for having conversations with new people so as he approached someone he knew, I just drifted off to look at a window.

Then, my father called me over to him. I wanted to "beam out" of the area like during a *Star Trek* movie. Instead, I had to charge up and present a kind smile and engage with the new person.

There is a problem with this situation. My desire not to engage in conversation because I was tired may have caused me to be seen as "aloof" by my father's friend.

The solution: Monitor your energy levels—in particular if you have introvert tendencies.

If you miss some sleep over a couple of days, do what you need to get more sleep and perhaps get some quiet time.

We need energy to stay approachable and be able to raise a genuine smile to our face.

3) Helpful not a doormat

A number people wince when they hear "victim-talk" that sounds like "The traffic did me in" and "Just my luck, I get the idiot barista that screws up my coffee and cake order."

Such negative talk sounds like a person is a "doormat" to the whole world. By doormat, we are talking about a person who lets people walk all over him or her.

This "doormat" idea relates to someone stuck in telling "woe is me/poor me" stories.

Confident people are NOT perceived as "doormats."

The solution is to carefully monitor the stories that you tell. Do *not* spread stories about how you have been exploited. Tell positive stories about how you help people to a healthy extent. You could say something like: "My friend Joe asked me to promote his new book on my Facebook page. I thought about it and talked it over with my marketing team member. I felt comfortable tweeting about his book. So I was able to help Joe that way."

Confident people set limits. Sure, they help people but they do *not* cross a line and become a "martyr."

The truth is: Some people who act like doormats eventually become so resentful that they lash out. You cannot trust someone like that.

Instead, you can trust confident people who take good care of themselves. Then they can be kind to others.

* * *

For many of us, a great personal brand would include doing what's necessary to be a trustworthy salesperson or business owner seeking funding.

Make a Presentation that Gets a Sale or Funding

A few years ago, I sat down to breakfast with a top Silicon Valley venture capitalist. We talked about presentations that succeed in getting funding. I mentioned how I prepared to write my book *Darkest Secrets of Making a Pitch for Film and Television: How You Can Get a Studio Executive, Producer, Name Actor or Private Investor to Say "Yes" to Your Project.*

"Frank, I sat through a number of pitches by top filmmakers, producers and directors to Silicon Valley investors, and I could *not* believe the mistakes they made. In fact, it inspired me to write my Pitch book. The filmmakers talked *at* the investors. On the other hand, I teach people to have a *dialogue* with the audience instead," I said.

"Nobody wants to have a dialogue. They just want to present," Frank agreed.

As we talked further, we noticed how the best people who pitch and the best salespeople are ones who ask great questions, listen and engage in a dialogue.

By the way, you make a great first impression when you ask questions and listen well!

We'll use the S.A.L.E. process:

S – Seek a dialogue

A – Ask questions

L – Listen well

E – End it well

1. Seek a dialogue

A principle that top salespeople know is: "The buyer convinces himself or herself. It's not what you say, it's what the *other person says.*"

So the good plan is to engage in a dialogue.

It requires that you prepare. To be effective in such a dialogue use my technique: *prepare for "Ten Questions You*

Don't Want to Answer." You come up with two answers per each question, for a total of twenty answers. Doing this will make you more prepared than the majority of people who give presentations (as I have observed from seeing hundreds of presentations).

2. Ask questions
You can ask questions like:
- So what's most important to you about ____?
- If my product works well for you, how will that improve your business?
- How do you see my product solving your XY problem?

When people answer questions like those above, they are convincing themselves to buy what you have to offer.

3. Listen well
Listening well includes three processes:
a) Remove Listening Blockers
b) Ask questions
c) Demonstrate that you heard and understand what the person is saying—and that you care about the person.

a) Remove Listening Blockers.

People tend to instantly judge what another person says. They also defend themselves, and they tend to tell a "me, too—one up" story. First, I will explain the "me too—one up" story. That is when someone says, "I'm so tired. I have a newborn." The unskillful person replies, "I can relate to that. I have newborn twins." That is a literal "one up" response.

Instead, when you see that you are judging or defending (or tempted to tell your story), ask a gentle question like:
- That sounds like it was a real problem. What did you do next?

- I hear how that caused some trouble. Is there something I can do to help with this situation?
- If things could get better, what would that look like?

b) *Ask questions*

What do people do naturally? Answer questions all day. The skill we want to develop is to ask "gentle questions" (which are those questions that are easy to answer and often fun to answer).

You can ask questions like:

- So what are you hoping my product/service will accomplish for you?
- What's most important to you about how my product/service does ____?

c) *Demonstrate that you heard and understand what the person is saying—and that you care about the person.*

Listening well is not just about keeping your mouth shut. It is really about assuring the other person that you truly understand her situation and that you care about her.

We accomplish this by saying things like:

- I heard you to say that XY is most important to you. Do I have that about right?
- Let me see if I fully understand. If XY does not happen, then it will cause you a ____ problem. Is there anything else that has you concerned?

You "say back" what you heard, AND you open the door for the person to further clarify her position.

I know that this can be powerful. I have shared with my family: "I realized that when I repeat myself; subconsciously I do *not* feel that I have been heard."

So when a family member says back what he or she heard me to say, I can feel that I was truly heard. That feels great!

When your prospective client *knows* that you care and understand his situation, you are so close to completing a transaction or getting your funding.

4. End it well

I train clients to end their presentation in a powerful, convincing manner.

They learn to say:

"In a moment, I can take a couple of questions and then I will summarize.

Who has the first question?

[My client answers the question(s).]

Who has the last question?

[My client answers the question.]

And now I will summarize."

At this point, my client provides a summary of the important details. The listeners feel the real value of the product/service.

Finally, my client closes the presentation with:

"Because of [Reason #1] and [Reason #2], I encourage you to please say *yes* to [funding our project]."

I have learned that putting the word "yes" into the room can get you a positive response.

The first time this worked for me is when I was in an audition for a commercial.

I said, "I hope you say *Yes* for me to be in your commercial." I began nodding.

The producer nodded. He looked to his team member on the left and his other team member on the right. They nodded, too.

The producer said, "Yes. We want you to be in the commercial."

Use the S.AL.E. methods:

S – Seek a dialogue

A – Ask questions

L – Listen well

E – End it well

Getting a *yes* response is not about pushing. It is really about facilitating the process so the prospective client speaks up and convinces himself or herself.

* * *

To really develop a powerful personal brand, you need great personal testimonials. Now, Patricia Fripp emphasizes the value of such testimonials.

Harness The Power of
Third-Party Endorsements
by Patricia Fripp, CSP, CPAE

A third-party endorsement is alchemy of sorts, taking hours of conversation and interaction and condensing it into a couple of sentences. **You cannot and must not lie when sharing third-party endorsement client stories, but you can condense a conversation. You can even dramatize an endorsement story as long as it is authentic and emotionally true.**

So, think of one of your good clients. They are listed on your website, and you already use them as a reference. Now, take the next step—call them and **ask this question, "Do you remember when we first did business; can you** remember what your major challenge was or why you chose us out of the three competitors?"

Listen carefully, because your clients will always give you the most compelling language. Get their exact words about their situation and the solution. When it comes time to incorporate a third-party story into your sales presentation or conversation, **you will say: "Based on my X years experience with clients of your size and complexity, this reminds me of what we did for Client Y. When we first talked to them they said they were having a problem with X. What we did, as we will do for you, was to offer eight options, six of which were just what they were looking for. As a result, they were successful in accomplishing [major goal]."**

Again, the situation and the success always need to be in your happy client's actual words. Rather than saying, "We exceeded their expectations with our creativity and speed," **it is much more effective to say, "If you were to call Client Y, she would tell you, 'We didn't believe it was possible for a company to come in this fast, have this impact, and not inconvenience our place of business. They exceeded our expectations across the board.'"** It's a small tweak to the language, but presenting the third-party perspective is dramatically far more powerful and persuasive.

Patricia Fripp, CSP, CPAE improves business one presentation at a time. Hers and yours! She is a Hall of Fame award-winning speaker, sales presentation skills trainer, and in-demand executive speech coach. *Meetings and Conventions* magazine named her "One of the 10 most electrifying speakers in North America." *Kiplinger's Personal Finance* wrote, "Patricia Fripp's speaking skills training is one of the best ways to invest in you." Through www.FrippVT.com her highly interactive virtual training platform she offers a shortcut to sales and presentation success.

Patricia is trusted by clients such as Microsoft, ADP, Visa, Genentech, Wounded Warrior Project, and the American Payroll Association.

Fripp was the first woman to be President of the National Speakers Association and is a partner in World Champions' Edge speaking community. Their Lady & the Champs Speakers' Conference attracts attendees worldwide.

www.fripp.com

* * *

A powerful personal brand is enhanced when you speak with positive impact. Now, we will learn from Patricia Fripp's insights about arranging your words for greater impact.

Impact Phrases—Are You Throwing Away Your Opportunities?
by Patricia Fripp, CSP, CPAE

If it is your goal to be a great communicator, make it your goal to be remembered and repeated. One approach to making your ideas more memorable is to **pay close attention to the way you order your words and phrases, even within a single sentence.** Audiences are most able to engage with us when we present information in a natural progression which helps them "see" what we are attempting to convey. **Like a miniature story, a single well-crafted sentence can draw your audience in, enabling them to connect both intellectually and emotionally as they follow your narrative to its conclusion.**

Scene-setting information, such as a date, time, and place, should always come at the beginning of a sentence as a "setup phrase." This helps the audience visualize what you are saying. **Save the end of your sentence for the most significant piece of information you intend to deliver, your "impact phrase."** If your impact phrase is at the beginning of your sentence, you and your audience may gloss over it, throwing away your opportunity to make your idea or point "stick" with your audience.

For example, if we were to turn on CNN, we might hear a sentence that sounded like this, "President Obama delivered a speech on healthcare at Yale University yesterday."

If this sentence were a part of your presentation, **I would recommend that you say,** "Yesterday.... (Immediately establishes the context of recent history.) ...at Yale University... (Sets the place. I imagine beautiful grounds, nice buildings.) ...President Obama... (We easily recognize who that is.) ...delivered a speech on healthcare."

You might say, "Your company had its best sales year ever in 1956."

You would have more impact on your audience if you said, "In 1956... (Let your audience slip into the time frame; they can almost see the tail fins on the Chevys.) ....your company had its best sales year ever."

Before... "...to celebrate your accomplishments in 2014."
Fripped... "...to celebrate your 2014 **accomplishments.**"

Before... "This will be our focus for the next two days."
Fripped... "For the next two days, this will be **our focus**."

Small changes can make a big difference. **Consider how you might rearrange words within your presentation for a greater impact on your audience.**

Patricia Fripp, CSP, CPAE improves business one presentation at a time. Hers and yours! She is a Hall of Fame award-winning speaker, sales presentation skills trainer, and in-demand executive speech coach. *Meetings and Conventions* magazine named her "One of the 10 most electrifying speakers in North America." *Kiplinger's Personal Finance* wrote, "Patricia Fripp's speaking skills training is one of the best ways to invest in you." Through www.FrippVT.com her highly interactive virtual training platform she offers a shortcut to sales and presentation success. Patricia is trusted by clients such as Microsoft, ADP, Visa, Genentech, Wounded Warrior Project, and the American Payroll Association.

Fripp was the first woman to be President of the National Speakers Association and is a partner in World Champions' Edge speaking community. Their Lady & the Champs Speakers' Conference attracts attendees worldwide.

www.frippvt.com, prfripp@fripp.com, (415)753-6556

Patricia Fripp, Improving business one presentation at a time.

Book Five:
Make a Great First Impression Online

Make a Great First Impression Online

Social media can speed up the process of connecting with new people. In fact, your blog, for example, can work for you while you're asleep. Think of your pages at Linkedin, Facebook, Google+, Pinterest, Twitter, Tumbler and more as 24/7 ambassadors building your personal brand.

We'll use the S.O.C.I.A.L process:

S – Stay safe

O – Offer help

C - Collaborate

I – Include "thinkspace"

A – Ask "how are things going?"

L – Listen and develop your "Tribe" (blogging)

1. Stay safe

I have a colleague who does not include her birthday on Facebook. She tells me, "A person's birthday is one of the points that companies use to identify you. If you do not post your birthday around, you're safer from identity theft."

Keeping your reputation safe in order to make yourself attractive to employers or clients is vital when it comes to your online presence. Sometimes, my clients talk about photos on their Facebook pages. It is cited in numerous places that employers check Facebook pages to see if someone "drinks too much" or is a "party animal." Each photo you share either builds your positive personal brand or breaks it down. You can use this principle: *If in doubt, leave it out.*

2. Offer help

Often, when I connect with someone who is new to writing, I offer an article I wrote entitled "How You Can Take Suffering Out of Writing." I have full credibility to offer such advice since I have written 26 books. More than that, I'm offering the article to relieve a new writer of some painful times.

If nothing comes of my gesture with the article, I am fine with that because I am putting more good into the world.

This is a helpful approach. Look upon offering free blog articles or free reports as part of your kind and friendly way of being in the world.

On several occasions, I have approached top authors and said, "I really appreciate your work. May I promote your work from the pages of my next book? Your guest article will have your biography and website immediately with your article." More than twenty authors have said *yes*. They find that more free publicity is a gift to them.

3. Collaborate

One time I saw that my blog page was not registering Facebook shares. I asked a friend online if he would help me do an experiment: Would he be okay if I posted on his Facebook wall a message with a link to my blog article? Then we would see if my blog page would register the Facebook share.

In gently asking, I was inviting my friend to *collaborate* with me in discovering details of the situation. We were both curious as to the outcome.

Special Forms of Collaborating: Joint Ventures and Using Web Site Ranking Tools

A significant form of collaborating is to form a *joint venture* with others who have esubscriber lists. We see this happen often in the publishing world. For example, I have teamed up with other authors, and for different campaigns, authors promote each others' books and audio programs. Working with other authors has helped my books serve people in 15 countries.

Although a number of people would not look upon a Web Site Ranking Tool (like http://nibbler.silktide.com/) as a "collaborator," I note that such a Ranking Tool truly helps me see how well my various websites are doing in terms of reaching out to more people in the social media sphere.

Collaborating through LinkedIn, Google+, Twitter, Facebook, Pinterest, WordPress and YouTube

I will now share some brief thoughts and methods for some of the significant social media websites.

Linkedin

People serious about their careers have a personal page on Linkedin and they join groups. Once you join a group you can send a message to any group member. A number of people post a question to the group and find that they are in contact with people who are the top of an industry and who respond to their inquiry.

Secondly, consider starting your own group.

At the moment I have two groups:

- Executive Public Speaking and Communication Power (anyone can sign up)
- Take Flight (a group for my former

college/graduate students to assist them with networking)

When you have your own group, you can post messages that reference your blog articles. In this way, each week you can keep yourself in group members' minds—as Linkedin sends an email to invite group members to view your posted message.

Google+

Some people scoff about Google+ but my circle of contacts at Google+ grows every week. You can also set up your own group (known as a Community). My group is "Create Your Best Life – Charisma and Confidence" which arose from my book, *Create Your Best Life: Unleash Your Charisma and Confidence to Change the World*. I also post links to my blog articles at a number of other Communities. When you set up a Google+ comm unity (and a Linkedin group), you make it easier for people to find you.

Twitter

Twitter is another website that can help you connect with top people in your industry. You can post a tweet every week when you post a new blog post.

Facebook

One of my colleagues told me that she had success with a Facebook ad. I suggest caution about paying for ads. Her results may be an anomaly because she was starting from a strong position. She had already had a well-received book and a strong esubscriber list, a well-received blog and comments from many happy clients. The place to start is to gather testimonials from delighted clients.

Facebook also often changes their rules. So I suggest you consult appropriate websites to see the recent articles about how Facebook is operating at the time you are reading this book.

I have a number of Facebook contacts who share my blog articles by placing links on their Facebook wall. I'm grateful for that.

Pinterest

One of my clients told me that her blog (operated on the WordPress platform) gets most of its referrals from Pinterest. Her topic relates to young women and so that fits with Pinterest. It is reported that 80% of Pinterest users are women and there are over 70 million Pinterest users.

WordPress

I advise my clients to use WordPress as the foundation of their blog. I like that WordPress has tools that show you how many views you are getting from which countries on which particular pages of your website (plus other analytics on board).

Here are two interesting facts:

- 48% of Technorati's Top 100 Blogs Are Managed With WordPress
- WordPress-Related Keywords Score 37 Million Searches Per Month

WordPress has many standard elements that make it interface well with the rest of the Internet. As noted above, the Keywords pull searches. Also, the headers of pages are coded in such a way that your website ranks higher. Those are just a few of the favorable elements of WordPress.

Many people find WordPress to be intuitive and user-friendly.

I have used WordPress for my
BeHeardandBeTrusted.com blog for years.

YouTube

I find YouTube really helpful when I am on the phone with a new contact. I ask, "Are you online?" . . . "How about you see a one minute video connected to my graphic novel *Jack AngelSword*. It has footage at a Mayan Ruin and I'm doing helmet diving." People most often say *yes.* A one minute video sounds brief enough.

Some months ago, I was connecting with a literary agent. Within minutes of my sending him the link to my *Jack AngelSword* video, he contacted me. Video is powerful. At the moment, I have 18 videos in my YouTube channel—with more on the way.

Some people make their YouTube channel their livelihood. If one has an attractive personality and topics, one can get people to donate to support one's channel. A number of YouTube personalities use Patreon.com as the vehicle to gather monthly donations from their fans.

Some people note that one can make money from YouTube directly. It's reported that one million views on YouTube translates to about $3,000 from AdSense, YouTube's ad revenue sharing program.

4. Include "thinkspace"

A friend of mine asked me what to do about someone asking for funds. My first response was: "Take some time. That is, give yourself 'thinkspace.' It's best to pause and think through before you do something."

After some consideration and conversations, my friend replied to someone on Facebook requesting funds with "I'm concerned about your situation. I'm sad to report that my funds are already going to help family members with trouble."

It is tempting to reply quickly to people on Facebook (and other websites) to simply get the "work over with," but you could cause more trouble and lose more time!

So pause. Get some thinkspace. And talk through your options with people whom you trust.

5. Ask "how are things going?"

I have learned that asking a neutral "How are things going?" works in many situations. It is not too personal, and we avoid "How are you?"

I have even seen that some people do *not* respond well to "What are you looking forward to?" Why? The tough thing about social media is you have no idea (no ability to hear a voice or see a person's face during a gmail-chat for example) what mood the person is in. So a question may strike the person at 2 AM in the morning after their tough day. They feel like you are prying or putting them in the hot seat. So I find a neutral "How are things going?" as a suitable start for a chat session.

6. Listen and develop your "Tribe" (blogging)

Just like in-person, I devote much time online to listening to the other person. I have noted that people like to complain and vent. So I listen.

To really develop your influence, consider launching your own blog. Then people who value your thoughts will gather and invite others to read your blog articles. You will see your Tribe form.

A tribe is a group of people connected to one another, connected to a leader, and connected to an idea. . . .A group needs only two things to be a tribe: a shared interest and a way to communicate.

– Seth Godin

One of my clients started from zero fans and then (via my guidance), she now has blog visitors from over 141 countries. This helped her get the attention of a senior acquisitions editor at a major publishing company.

When it comes to choosing what to blog about it's valuable to be *specific* in your target market.

Here are two great examples of people who started with blog articles that became best-selling books:

- blog: gretchenrubin.com The resulting book, *The Happiness Project* by Gretchen Rubin
- blog: the Julie/Julia Project The resulting book, *Julie and Julia: 365 Days, 524 Recipes, 1 Tiny Apartment Kitchen* (It inspired the 2009 feature film starring Meryl Streep and Amy Adams—which had a budget of $40 million and earned $129.5 million)

The process is now referred to as "blog your book."

Use the S.O.C.I.A.L process:

S – Stay safe

O – Offer help

C - Collaborate

I – Include "thinkspace"

A – Ask "how are things going?"

L – Listen and develop your "Tribe" (blogging)

Working with social media does NOT take the place of in-person networking, but it can be a powerful addition.

Because of social media, I have fans in a number of countries and I see that my books sell in several countries.

How would your business life improve if you expanded your efforts related to social media?

Even posting two messages a day can help you build your following. Such action is *better than zero.*

* * *

When you are active in social media, you will have thousands of contacts. Some will become friends. Others will bring some negativity to you life. This leads our discussion in an important direction . . .

The Hidden Truth About Power Networking

"This conversation was largely useless to me," Reginald said.

This was a stunning remark since yet again I had done a lot of listening to my friend. Still, I replied, "I don't do useless things. I won't be calling you. If you have an emergency, you can call me. I wish you the best. Is there anything else?"

"No."

"Many blessings to you," I said. That was the end of my phone conversation with Reginald.

I have not talked with him for years, and my life has been better for it.

(There had been other signs that the relationship was coming to an end, but nothing made it more clear than Reginald's use of the words "largely useless.")

There is a side to networking that some authors do not emphasize: **The hidden truth is that it is important to heed when someone is *not* a fit for our circle of contacts.**

I recall Gabrielle Reece's (Olympic athlete, model and mother) powerful comment: "30% of the people will love you. 30% will hate you, and 30% couldn't care less."

Someone may be a good part of your life for some years, but then you drift apart. At one point, Oprah Winfrey interviewed a number of people and asked, "What do you know for sure?"

My reply would be: "I know for sure that a new chapter of my life can start on any day."

That day, when I bid Reginald goodbye, a new chapter of my life without Reginald began.

To save your precious time, it is important to heed the clues and realize when someone (even a family member) relates to you as a "30% hates you" or "30% couldn't care less."

If you realize that the person is, for whatever reason, not on your side then let him or her drift away.

I have been a fiercely loyal friend who listened so diligently to friends whom I have known for over two decades. However, in the case of Reginald, I heeded the "largely useless" clue and turned my time and attention to those people who are positive.

Surround yourself with only people who are going to lift you higher. - Oprah Winfrey

Now it's your turn.

Are there a couple of people who do *not* lift you higher? Is it time to let them drift out of your life?

In Power Networking, you need to concentrate on positive people who naturally connect with you.

Save your personal time and energy.

Even with certain family members, you might choose to reduce the amount of time that you are exposed to them.

As you do better and better in life, some people are going to feel uncomfortable around you. Do yourself and them a favor: let them drift away.

Although it can be hard to let go of some people, you will do better when you create a form of "vacuum." When there is space, friendly people and more opportunities can rush into your life.

Your life is valuable. Fill it with the people who care

about that value.

* * *

We just covered the difficulty that people experience when they have to let go of someone in their circle of contacts. Now, we will explore the power of letting go.

Use the Amazing Power of "Let Go"

The sharp pain in my back felt like I was being cut in half.

This was the worst pain I had felt in my life—which includes being hit in the chest by a truck.

I was having the first severe back spasm of my life. And then another spasm happened. My back arched and the pain had me on the verge of throwing up.

I could *not* get out of bed.

This experience taught me something—dramatically—that I had not learned in another form.

To get my back and abdominal muscles to stop clenching, I told myself: "Let go, let go, let go."

I had to be flexible and find a new way to get out of bed that avoided using my back and abdominal muscles. It involved crawling and using my arms.

A remarkable irony here was I needed two powers: "Let go" and "Whatever it takes."

I had to do whatever it took to get out of bed.

Secondly, I had to let go or I'd collapse in agony.

* * *

When working with clients, I have often emphasized the power of ALF – adapt, learn, flex. When I say, "flex" I'm referencing the idea of "being flexible."

Now, it's your turn.

Where in your life do you need to let go?

Is there someone who is not acting in a way you prefer? Are you hoping that they will change? Is it possible that you may need to move on?

Or is the person a family member (like an elderly relative) who is simply mean and negative? And, do you need to reduce your time in their presence?

Secondly . . .

Is there something that you want that requires you to make a deeper level of commitment? Do you need to finally vow, "I'll do whatever it takes"?

Flexibility and commitment . . . and taking effective action will help you rise to new and better levels of success and happiness.

It may not be easy. But it is certainly worth the effort involved.

Book Six:
Become Strong and Enhance Your Networking (includes special Secrets for Introverts)

Power networking takes significant personal energy. This section will help you become stronger.

We will cover these topics:

1) Secrets for Introverts to Do Well with In-Person Networking
2) How Introverts Can Do Well When Others Want Them to "Talk Faster"
3) Introverts as Excellent Public Speakers
4) Know the One Thing and Massively Improve Your Life!
5) Stop Chasing the Wind; Experience Your Hidden Happiness
6) Better than You Imagined – Secrets to Create Your Best Life
7) Ignite Your Inner Badass and Win!
8) Do NOT Let Anyone Bleed the Life Out of You!
9) Free Yourself from Fear
10) Bounce Back from a Low Time
11) Make This Year Great for You: The TRUTH on How You Can Keep Going While Others Quit
12) Believe in Yourself, Take Action–Do NOT Let Anyone Hold You Back!

Secrets for Introverts to Do Well with In-Person Networking

Are you an introvert? There are a lot of guesses and theories floating about as to what an introvert really is. Ask yourself this question: "Do you need to recharge your personal energy by having some time *away* from others?" You might have a few "introvert tendencies."

Now, we'll explore the I.N.T.R.O. process to help you gear up for networking events:

I – Invest in building your energy
N – Nurture your lines before an event
T – Target reasonable goals
R – Recover as you go along
O – Organize support

1. Invest in building your energy

Many extroverts *like* to go to social gatherings because they get a rush of new personal energy. On the other hand, many introverts hesitate about going to an in-person networking event because they feel the need to "power-up" to be ready to talk with people.

Some introverts look upon going to an event as terrible duty that they must endure to try to get business. Such an experience can be self-defeating. *The solution* is to consciously decide to take action to build up your energy. How? For introverts, time alone can be "battery-charging."

For example, I have some introvert tendencies so I find that time with music and assembling a jigsaw puzzle as relaxing and energy-restoring. Focus on whatever you enjoy doing—that builds your energy—and do it! You owe it to yourself in building a better you. Activities you enjoy to *recharge* are key in helping you succeed with opportunities that might otherwise appear daunting.

But this is not all when it comes to investing your focus and effort. Another point is: Guard your personal energy before an event. That is, avoid going to a meeting in the afternoon before an evening networking event. Take care of yourself. You really need more personal energy to be at your best at the networking event.

2. Nurture your lines before an event

What causes you to be most nervous? Is it that you don't know your words (your lines) before you step into the room of an event?

I emphasize with my clients to "nurture your lines;" and by this I mean for you to take a higher level approach: Rehearse what you will say. (Often it helps to gain coaching). With my clients on the phone, I guide them through *Dynamic Rehearsal*. I take on the role of the other person and the client rehearses how she'll speak and respond to the other person.

Rehearsal gives you a real benefit: If You KNOW that you *know* how to perform better, your confidence is enhanced.

3. Target reasonable goals

Some people have a mistaken notion that one has to stay for hours at an event and give out 30 business cards.

Instead, it's better to target reasonable goals like: "Stay for 1 hour. Have 5 good conversations. Gain 4 business cards."

4. Recover as you go along

After you complete one conversation, you might find it helpful to take a breather—a short break. You could step outside the room and get a bit of fresh air. You could get a drink of water. If you're an introvert, support yourself and realize that it is taking personal energy for you to interact with each person at the event. Take a break. Renew your energy.

5. Organize support

Consider bringing a friend or supportive family member to the event. You can "retreat" to your friend for support. You can even get a bit of encouragement. You might say, "I just talked with the second person of five that I'm aiming for." Your friend says, "Good for you! Here, have a bite of this hors d'oeuvre."

Now, a bit refreshed, you take leave of your friend and step over to talk with a third person.

Or you could still feel some support by texting or calling a friend on your cell phone.

*   *   *

Many introverts find that they have different skills and positive tendencies than others (including extroverts).

A number of introverts are good listeners. Many are quite thoughtful. Several introverts make others feel comfortable because they are listening and not battling for the limelight in the conversation.

Use the I.N.T.R.O. process:

I – Invest in building your energy

N – Nurture your lines before an event

T – Target reasonable goals

R – Recover as you go along

O – Organize support

Stop fighting any introvert tendencies you may have. Give yourself a break. Instead, support yourself and let go of berating yourself for being different from extroverts. Be sure to renew your personal energy.

There are extroverts longing to have a kind introvert listen to them.

You can be that supportive person.

And often you'll find that you're building a good, new connection.

How Introverts Can Do Well When Others Want Them to "Talk Faster"

Some introverts say, "I don't like to meet new people at networking events because people are expecting me to respond quickly. Instead, I like to think through my responses."

One way an introvert can deal with this pressure to reply quickly is to say: "I've not thought of that quite that way before. I might need to pause for a moment. I want my response to be useful to our conversation."

For many of us, simply saying the above comment gives us more time to think of our next reply. Why? On average, people's brain tends to work at 700 words a minute, so your brain is already looking for your answer to a question. You are just giving it more time.

There is strategy involved with saying, "I might need to pause for a moment." You are letting the other person know what *you* are doing, and you're not asking the other person to do something.

Another alternative is the following form of response: "I have two replies to your question."

"Yes?" asks the other person.

"I have my first impression, and then there's my reply that's based on my pausing and considering the details a bit longer. I prefer thinking about a question for a moment or two."

It is best to avoid using the above methods too much, but they *can* be used sparingly and well.

Introverts as Excellent Public Speakers

My leg shook like a hummingbird's wings while I played the piano for thirty-one seniors at a retirement home. As my little nine-year-old hands danced on the keyboard, I was terrified of making a mistake or having my shaking foot slip off piano's sustain pedal. One slip and a big THUD sound would crash the piano recital.

About twenty years later, I stood up from my chair in the middle of an audience of 500 people and asked questions of the multi-millionaire speaker. The speaker gave me a pointed critique of my business card. I was learning, but then I noticed that my right leg was shaking violently. Oh!— it was back: my hummingbird-flutter leg.

Soon I sat down. I asked my girlfriend about how I did. She said, "You did well." She had *not* noticed my shaking leg. This alerted me to the fact that on the inside one can be nervous, but *you can simultaneously look professional on the outside.*

This is an important distinction. Every year I help new speakers use methods to do well when giving a speech.

Introverts have additional challenges when it comes to giving a speech. To overcome such challenges, we will use the A.I.M. process:

A – Align with friendly faces
I – Increase one-to-one conversations
M – Make moments to "think through"

1. Align with friendly faces

Introduce yourself to audience members *before* your give your speech. Say, "Hi. I'm _____, and I'm you're speaker for today. I'm wondering if you came up with a question when you first learned of the title of today's speech. What topic, if I can address it, would really help you?" Take a few notes as the person talks, and ask for the person's name.

Meet around five people. Then when you are on stage, you will already have friendly faces in the audience. You can address these individuals and the process will be more like talking to one person at a time.

In fact, you can say, "Before this presentation, I was talking with a number of you, and Susan mentioned the XYZ project and how . . . "

This builds a better connection with the audience.

2. Increase one-to-one conversations

A number of introverts have told me, "I'm fine when talking to one person, but I'm thrown off when I speak to a group." My answer is: Approach your speech as a series of one-to-one conversations. Pick someone to talk with on the right side of the room, and pick one from the middle and one from the left side. The helpful phenomenon is that when you speak to one person, the people in front of and behind that person feel like you're talking to them, too.

By the way, if anyone looks tired or distracted, simply shift your eyes to someone else. You are likely to find someone who resonates with your presentation. Talk to that person.

3. Make moments to "think through"

Introverts often feel extra pressure while they give a speech. Many say, "I don't like to give a hasty answer to someone's question. I prefer to think through a topic and then give a well-thought out answer."

This makes sense since many introverts treasure alone time to do some research and find well-supported answers.

We will cover four methods so that you can think through your answer.

Method #1: Take a drink of water. While you have some water, you can think about the question and formulate your answer. (Also, reach for the water, if your mind goes blank for a moment. The water buys you some time.)

Method #2: Say, "I'll need to pause for a moment. I want my answer to be useful to you."

Method #3: Say, "I haven't looked at it quite that way before. I'll need to pause for a moment. I want my answer to be helpful to you."

Method #4: Say, "I like to give thoughtful answers. So first, I'll give you an impression. And then I'll talk about what I find to be important considerations when we talk about _____. In fact, I'll suggest what a good solution would include..."

The above phrases help you have time to think through your answer. Memorize these phrases so you can easily say them. Simultaneously, your mind will work at 700 words a minute to find a good answer.

As an introvert, take advantage of your ability to think deeply. Just give yourself some more time.

Finally, here is an important observation. When you're speaking, a pause seems longer. But to the audience, a pause is not that long because they are thinking and trying to keep up with you. The material is all new to them. Or at least, they are learning about your point of view.

They want you to pause. They want to hear smart and thought through details.

Good. As an introvert, you provide the clarity the audience craves.

When you do that you are perceived as an expert, and it is easier to get more clients.

Know the One Thing and Massively Improve Your Life!

The workshop attendee's question rang through my meeting room. I had just read it out loud: "If there is one thing you want us to gain from this workshop, what would it be?"

Before I could answer the question, I had to set the scene. I replied, "Just after I graduated from college, I had to raise funds for my first feature film. There was no Facebook, Kickstarter, Linkedin or Amazon.com. I didn't know what to do. I did not live in Los Angeles. I was in a small town in Northern California. I was desperate. I started writing the screenplay late at night and then slept through the day. Then I thought, 'Oh – 5pm. So I don't need to call anybody today.' Remember, I was desperate and I didn't know how to raise money*."

* This desperation about how to raise funds for filmmaking inspired me, years later, to write my book *Darkest Secrets of Making a Pitch for Film and Television: How You Can Get a Studio Executive, Producer, Name Actor or Private Investor to Say "Yes" to Your Project*

I looked into the eyes of the audience. "From that desperate time, I made a decision **to study everyday and make myself ready** for the next unknown, tough things to happen in my life."

"So what I want you to get from this workshop is to learn the methods and strategies. So you get strong. So you can do well in your career."

"The **one thing** I want you to take from this workshop is: **You need preparation to be strong so you can face the unknowns in life.**"

"Put effort into this workshop. Make this workshop like an orange that you squeeze and get the juice."

* * *

Now, I invite you to get some real value from this article. Grab your journal or a sheet of paper and write answers to these questions:

- What's One Thing you can do to prepare?
- What's One Thing you can rehearse?
- What's One Thing you need to learn?

And here is the vital question: **What is the One Thing you will do and *when* this week?**

Focus. Prepare. Rehearse. Take action. Repeat.

Your life will improve, often beyond your first imaginings.

Stop Chasing the Wind; Experience Your Hidden Happiness

This was the moment—my first feature film was done! In the studio, I turned to my team and their smiles centered on "Done! Finally!" But I did not feel the big, happy moment. Really—I was tired. On some level, I felt relieved.

I learned something powerful.

I learned to "stop chasing the wind" and I learned about "hidden happiness."

When I was making my first feature film, I was a true believer: we were making an uplifting film. And yes, I found that the finished film did make some people feel good. I remember sitting on a couch. In San Francisco, the couch shook and I thought I was experiencing an earthquake. No, my father was laughing at the right moment in my feature film. He shook with silent laughter and that caused the rumble in the couch. That was good.

I felt good when receiving a Polish fan's email. That was fun hearing about how he had seen my feature film on

Polish television.

I learned about "chasing the wind" in that what I have thought would be the big, happy moment did not happen. At least not how I imagined it.

And then I learned about "hidden happiness."

It was not about making big money. I'm an entrepreneur. Some of my projects have made a good cash flow. Other projects have not.

I discovered my "hidden happiness" is really **Connection.**

It is feeling connected as I write these words that you are reading.

It is feeling connected . . .

- when I'm on the set directing.

- when I'm talking with one of my illustrators who is improving a page of my graphic novel *Jack AngelSword.*

- when I'm helping my clients.

I also feel connected when I am answering a question while giving a speech to an audience of 697 people.

So to put it in a few words:

"Chasing the wind" is looking for that one big happy moment or that one moment feeling totally secure.

The hidden happiness is feeling connected.

I remember being on a spiritual retreat and flowing with martial arts moves under a canopy of bright stars (out in nature).

I felt connected with God and the universe.

I have learned there are *Three Elements of Experiencing Connection:* a) set the stage, b) rehearse and c) enter the moment fresh.

You may not be able to force a particular outcome. But you can *"set the stage."* You can take a walk with your sweetie on a beach or in the neighborhood and as a result maybe you will share a moment of laughter. That is how you "set the stage" in getting connected. The set up was taking a walk on the beach; the result was sharing a moment of laughter—a moment of personal connection.

As an artist and professional speaker, I know that when I *rehearse*, I can do better when I am on stage.

Finally, I have learned that *"entering the moment fresh"* helps me do better in a given instant. When I avoid letting any past feelings or any worries for the future interfere, then I can be fully present in this moment. This moment is where the real living happens.

I invite you to go directly toward happiness.

Where is it? *It's in Connection.*

Better than You Imagined – Secrets to Create Your Best Life

"Really? You think I can do that?!" Sam asked. I'd seen such a look on the face of a number of clients. It happens when I encourage clients to explore what they *really want in life.*

It's like the sun bursts through the clouds, and the clients feel the permission to express what's deep in their hearts.

Asking is the beginning of receiving. Make sure you don't go to the ocean with a teaspoon. At least take a bucket... - Jim Rohn

Living a life of joy, adventure and fulfillment is like going to the ocean with a bucket to collect a LOT of sea water. I'm talking about collecting a lot of experiences, resources and cooperation for your extraordinary life.

Unfortunately, a number of people I have talked with have apparently given up on living on the "fulfilling-my-dreams" level.

What is needed here is a *shift in mindset*. So will use the G.I.F.T. process:

G – get others involved
I – imagine better
F – focus
T – "trust-build"

1. Get others involved

I made my first film when I was nine years old. Immediately, I learned that there was a way to get people to participate in my projects. The answer was: "inviting people to have a good time."

Nothing is impossible for the man who doesn't have to do it himself. – A. H. Weiler

I learned that expressing appreciation and appropriately praising work helps people feel good about themselves, the team and the project.

2. Imagine better

This article is titled "Better than You Imagined." I have learned that to be a leader you need to first imagine something better, communicate that vision and then set the "playground" so people can do their best work.

Imagination is everything. It is the preview of life's coming attractions. – Albert Einstein

The leader is ahead of the team pointing in the direction of the positive vision. That takes imagination.

3. Focus

Focus is crucial for making a dream come true. I can come up with a book idea and with three editors (editing different sections simultaneously) finish a book in 90 days. How? I work on the project every day. That's focus.

One reason so few of us achieve what we truly want is that we never direct our focus; we never concentrate our power. Most people dabble their way through life, never deciding to master anything in particular. – Tony Robbins

Let others lead small lives, but not you. Let others argue over small things, but not you. Let others cry over small hurts, but not you. Let others leave their future in someone else's hands, but not you. – Jim Rohn

Focus on what you want and do NOT let fear shut you down. I have written about courage often in my books because I have learned that taking action often requires pressing on despite fear.

Focus on the "big good" and you will feel the personal energy to navigate through the "smaller bad." Make what you want more important than fear.

It's so important to me that I support clients, students and readers to expand their vision and efforts to create a joyful life that I wrote a book entitled: *Yes! Secrets for Your Best Life – Law of Attraction plus Hidden Power Increases Your Success and Happiness.*

Here I emphasize that focus is a crucial element of creating your best life.

The great majority of people are "wandering generalities" rather than "meaningful specifics." The fact is that you can't hit a target that you can't see. If you don't know where you are going, you will probably end up somewhere else. You have to have goals.

- Zig Ziglar

Unfortunately, a number of people have felt "burned by goal setting." Perhaps, they failed after setting New Year's Resolutions. Or they're afraid of looking foolish if they attain a goal but discover they do not want the particular lifestyle. Maybe they are simply afraid of the pain of disappointing themselves. Many may even think that focusing on goals reduces the flexibility to change or do others things, but this it hardly the case.

The truth is: Focus is crucial for making a dream come true. You still have flexibility. If you discover that your original goal no longer serves you. Change your approach.

When I first started in the film industry, I was focusing on one story at a time to become a success. In recent years though, I work on a series of graphic novels (for example, *Jack AngelSword*) because I know that Hollywood studios prefer franchises. Thus, I have changed my approach in achieving success. Is it different than what I originally started doing? Yes, but my goal and focus remain the same, and I work on my projects every day.

It is so important to me that I support clients, students, and readers to expand their vision and efforts to create a joyful life. For example, in the book I mentioned, *Yes! Secrets for Your Best Life*, I talk more about the process of focusing, and I emphasize that it takes work to do so. Too many people believe that focus is nothing more than concentrating your thoughts on a particular goal or desired outcome, but it also takes action. Focus also takes your willingness to act in order to achieve what you desire. Simply wanting something is not enough—You Must Act!

4. "Trust-build"

With trust, big things happen. People commit to doing a great job. People follow your lead.

What is one thing that can help you build trust? Listening.

I share with my clients: "When you're listening, you're winning."

Also, develop your own personal standards. Be a little early for appointments. Be careful about your promises and write them down in your calendar. Live in such a way that people can count on you.

When people trust you, they will offer you cooperation

and opportunities that untrustworthy people never hear about.

In a nutshell:

To create a life better than you imagined, develop good relationships and other people will help and make the projects more textured and literally better than you first imagined.

How fun!

Ignite Your Inner Badass and Win!

Well—this is a first. I don't usually use certain language like "badass." Why? Because I'm a trained speaker. I do NOT want to accidently trip over a cord when on stage during a speech and drop the f-bomb.

However, the phrase "Ignite Your Inner Badass" says the idea with truth and clarity.

There is a part of YOU that is naturally strong, decisive and will take no garbage!

We'll use the C.A.N. process:

C – Cancel apologizing for being YOU

A – Appreciate your strengths

N – Nurture yourself when others don't believe in you

1. Cancel apologizing for being YOU

Years ago, I had a particular friend "Bob" who would gather a group of friends at his home. I would say something and then, to tiptoe around Bob's feelings, I would diminish my comment by adding, "That's just me. I'm weird."

But then I reflected on this. I realized that diminishing my comment was actually diminishing myself. Something was off if I had to diminish myself while in Bob's presence.

The next morning at breakfast I said to the four people gathered, including Bob, "I've noticed that I've been saying 'that's just me, I'm weird,' and I am *through* with that. I'm not going to say 'weird,' anymore. I'm not going to diminish myself. Yes, I'm different. I'll answer to 'I'm different.'"

Recently, someone gave me pushback when it came up in conversation that I had written 26 books. This guy, "Sam," said, "Hey, I don't think you should tell people that."

I responded, "Well, writing IS one of my art forms. I made sure NOT to introduce myself and push the 26 books detail. But people were later talking about things they felt good about and I told the truth. I worked hard for each book. I earned them. And I enjoyed much of the writing each book."

My point here is: No matter what you say or what you do, someone is going to resist or criticize. **Do NOT apologize for being YOU.**

Sure, be tactful. No one wants to hear your resume or a monologue of your accomplishments.

But if you really like something ... I like *FROZEN* (the animated film). There! I said it.

. . . if you really like something you can express it in appropriate ways.

2. Appreciate your strengths

If you are going to feel like a badass and get something big done in this world, you are going to need to OWN your strengths.

People hire people who are confident in their own abilities. Work hard to develop your skills and then let people know what you can do to help them.

Sometimes, idealistic people are put off the whole business of networking as something tainted by flattery and the pursuit of selfish advantage. But virtue in obscurity is rewarded only in

heaven. To succeed in this world you have to be known to people.
– Sonia Sotomayor, First Latina Supreme Court Justice

For example, when it comes mentioning your fee (if you are a contractor), practice saying your fee with confidence and be sure to say it smoothly.

I teach my clients and students to use this phrase: "In the marketplace, my fee level is ..." They learn to say this in a matter-of-fact tone. No stuttering and no apology.

3. Nurture yourself when others don't believe in you

With my clients, I emphasize: *You need preparation to be strong to face the unknowns.*

At times, life can be truly hard on each individual.

Several years ago, someone asked Steven Spielberg, "How do you prepare to direct a feature film?"

"Go to the gym," Spielberg replied. His point being that we need physical endurance to do tough projects like directing a feature film.

I take Spielberg's point literally and I exercise everyday.

By the way, Spielberg and Harrison Ford shared the same personal trainer when Harrison Ford portrayed a younger Indiana Jones in the second feature film of the *Indiana Jones* series of films.

So getting exercise and sleep are necessary parts of being a badass. Have you noticed that you can get more done and be more decisive on the days you wake up from a good sleep? There is no fluke here.

One of my close friends is a sport psychologist to Olympic athletes. Do you think athletes are haphazard about their sleep? No! They are disciplined about it.

There are two types of pain you will go through in life, the pain of discipline and the pain of regret. Discipline weighs ounces while regret weighs tons. – Jim Rohn

Be so good they can't ignore you [and you'll succeed].
– Steve Martin

Do you want to be a badass and get what you want in life?

Then be sure to:

Cancel apologizing for being YOU

Appreciate your strengths

Nurture yourself when others don't believe in you

You do not need to use the word "badass."

You can say it to yourself—where it counts.

You could say out loud, "Yes. I do work to get things done. People can count on me."

If you act in a trustworthy manner, you are already making yourself extraordinary.

"Ordinary people" regularly arrive late for meetings, make promises they do not keep, and fail to do the extra work to STAND OUT from the crowd.

Let other people lead small lives, but not you. – Jim Rohn

If you want to be rich, you can't be normal. – Noah St. John

If you want to experience joy and fulfillment, you need to play full out—to be a badass.

"My writing career . . . was some kind of crisis where you up and change. . . . In my 30's I wanted to read something else. I wanted to show how the constructed, horrible racism was on the most vulnerable people: girls, black girls, poor girls. And it could really and truly hurt you. And no one I thought had written that book. Since I really wanted to read it, I thought I should write it."
– Toni Morrison, Pulitzer Prize-winner and Nobel Prize- winner

Find your voice.

Express yourself.

Experience *your* life to the fullest.

Do NOT Let Anyone Bleed the Life Out of You!

Bam! The train slammed into something; my knee hit the seat in front of me. And the passenger car violently tilted to the right. I had just experienced riding in a derailed train.

The train engineer had brought the train into the San Francisco train station too fast and the train had hit the *barrier* hard enough to toss train wheels off the track.

Unfortunately, there are a number of people who function like *"barriers"* throwing us off our track—the track of our best destiny.

I am here to help you know and say to yourself: "I AM strong."

We'll use the A.M. process:

A – Arrange empowering questions

M – Measure daily progress

1. Arrange empowering questions

Have you heard a close friend or family member say, "That won't work. Almost nobody can make a living at that!"

Sometimes in my life I have wanted to yell: "Do you know what the hell you're doing?! You're stepping on my soul. You're saying exactly what takes the life out of me. You're spitting on my hope!"

But I do not say this. Why?

Because whether this is a friend or family member, they do NOT understand what they are doing.

The truth is: Your destiny is YOUR own. Other people can**not** see the vision. They cannot feel what you want *deep in your heart.*

It is like you are listening to music that they cannot hear.

They do not understand that your heart cries out for something better—for you to live, truly live!

Do not let other people bleed the life out of you. Set up your defenses.

One way to do this is: Focus on *Empowering Questions* that include:

- How can I make this work?
- How can I show on a small scale what I can do? [Perhaps, place a short film on YouTube if you want to be a film director or actor.]
- How can I get coaching and some education in this area?
- How can I make some daily progress?

2. Measure daily progress

How do you get strong? Through *Daily Empowering Habits*—making some form of progress everyday.

A number of my clients use a **Daily Journal of Victories and Blessings**. In just three minutes, before they go to bed, they see all of the accomplishments and good moments of the day. That is, they write down the highlights of their day on the appropriate page.

Here is another example. I exercise everyday, and I log my daily progress. Years ago, I woke with a severe neck pain. Since that time, I do daily neck exercises.

More recently, I woke up with my first crippling back spasm. In response to that, I do back exercises every day. Now my back is better and stronger.

When you truly want to get stronger, you need to make yourself an "open system." By this I mean, you need to get new ideas and new coaching so you can do better than you did yesterday or last month.

Unfortunately, I know a number of people who are "closed systems"—they are done learning new things. They are rigid and judgmental. Nothing new can get in so they cannot get stronger.

As in the above example, I adapted to my back difficulty and I applied the advice of two physical therapists concerning my back exercises.

Now it's your turn.

In what area of your life is someone "bleeding you" of your personal energy?

Is there someone (maybe an elderly relative) who insults you repeatedly?

Is there some friend who simply does not believe you can improve your life situation.

Do not allow the person to drain your enthusiasm and hope away.

Become proactive. Focus on your Empowering Questions and Daily Empowering Habits.

What Empowering Habits can you begin today?

Experiment. Try new things and find out how to nurture yourself.

You will make sure there is one LESS miserable person in the world.

You will feel better and that will affect people around you.

It is a terrific trend to start.

Thank you.

Free Yourself from Fear

Want to release yourself from the shackles of fear? Would you like more fun in your life? Some of us have noticed that a number of activities which scared us at first become enjoyable. Skateboarding can be daunting until a young person gets comfortable with it. Since dealing with fear is a prime skill of successful people that I've interviewed, I will now share the F.U.N. process:

F – focus on something important

U – unleash rehearsal

N – nurture action

1. Focus on something important

I've learned that what you focus on makes all the difference between fear and engaging with the present moment—and doing well.

When I made my performing debut as a nine-year-old amateur pianist before 31 seniors in a retirement home, I was focused on one thing: *Fear* that I would make some stupid mistake on the piano!

My focus was on "How am I doing?! How am I doing?!"

This focus made me so afraid that my right leg vibrated like the wings of a humming bird. My fear rose to a fever pitch because I was terrified that my shaking leg would lead to my foot falling off the sustain pedal. This, in my 9-year-old mind, would be "death by embarrassment" because the pedal hitting the frame of the piano would cause a loud THUD sound. The seniors would think I was such a dummy.

Along my journey, I learned to overcome such fear and I have become a professional speaker addressing audiences of over 657 people.

In my years of being coached, rehearsing and speaking, I've learned to Focus on Something More Important: serving the audience.

So I have transformed my thought process from "How am I doing?" to "How are YOU doing?"

If tomorrow I was playing the piano and my foot fell off the sustain pedal and a big THUD sound crashed my performance, I would mildly say to the audience: "Oh. That's new."

My response might earn a chuckle or two, and I would move on knowing that the audience was right there with me.

With this example, I'm talking about choosing your focus. Make something more important than your fear.

Courage is not the absence of fear but rather the judgment that something is more important than fear. – Meg Cabot

Now, it's your turn.

What could be more important than fear in your life?

How can you focus on what really matters to you? And would you consider getting coaching so you can improve your skills?

2. Unleash rehearsal

It's important that you *know* that you know how to do something. You get to that point knowing deep in your heart through two things: coaching and rehearsal.

Your next decision plus action can release you from the past.

– Tom Marcoux

Decide to get coaching. Decide to rehearse. Then you truly quiet down fear.

3. Nurture action

Do the thing you fear and the death of fear is certain.

– Ralph Waldo Emerson

After years of addressing audiences, including MBA students at Stanford University, high tech people at the National Association of Broadcasters Conference and more, I'm ready to deal with any mishap while I'm speaking on stage. I won't freeze up and feel terrible. I might just say, "Oh. I need a moment. I want my next comment to be really useful to you."

I'm *not* trying to appear perfect. In this way, I focus NOT on my ego-needs, but on serving the audience.

I've taken a lot of action by speaking before an audience nearly every week of the year. All of that action has helped me improve.

One time, on stage, I was speaking with such enthusiasm that I found myself teetering on the edge of the stage—just about to fall off.

No problem. I just said, "Oh! That's exciting!"

I shared a laugh with my audience and we moved forward in our conversation.

Do I ever get nervous and feel my shyness rise up? Yes. Then I use it as a sign that it's time for me to rehearse.

I share with my clients this idea:

Picture a kind grandmother encouraging you and saying, "Feeling fear? Rehearse my dear."

Now it's your turn.

How can you rehearse and concentrate on something you want so much that fear can quiet down and be put "into a drawer."

I'm not talking about erasing fear. Use the fear as energy to get you to rehearse.

I'm not afraid of storms, for I'm learning how to sail my ship.

– Louisa May Alcott

Life is a journey in which we explore new chapters and find new and better ways to sail.

Keep learning; keep sailing.

Bounce Back from a Low Time

Years ago, my father and I had a Christmas Eve tradition: We'd go to a bookstore. Back then, it was a special treat for me because I was on such a tight budget that stepping into a bookstore with the opportunity to pick any book for my Christmas gift was a warm and delightful opportunity. I felt real support.

In recent years, that tradition vanished. Why? Nearly 80 years old, my father has become bitter and he has thrown away that tradition.

I feel sad when I focus on the loss of this Christmas Eve tradition. Then, with my next thought, I remind myself: *"I'm grateful for that earlier chapter of my life."*

I've shared a number of steps with my clients for shifting gears and doing well even when we face some low mood times. We'll use the S.T.E.P. process, also known as "take a step forward."

S – Seek positive energy

T – Tell people who care

E – Expand from your "negative focus"

P – Pinpoint your purpose

1. Seek positive energy

Make a conscious choice to seek positive energy; you need it. You need to make a shift in focus. You are *not* going to get positive energy from doing what you've been doing or thinking the same thoughts repeatedly. A University of Pennsylvania study found that people tend to think 50,000 thoughts per day and 70% of them are negative. Stop that! Consciously turn the direction of your thoughts.

For example, I remember years ago when I endured the ending of a nearly 8 year relationship, I was devastated. Fortunately, I realized that I needed a change of scenery and thoughts. So I went with a friend to see Disney's animated *Pocahontas*, and I cried during the song/sequence "Colors of the Wind." What a relief!

Two things happened: I released some pent up feelings and I also enjoyed the humor, romance and artistry of that film.

I have had an appreciation for that film ever since. When I felt better, I became more productive.

Now it's your turn.

How can you do something different to experience some positive energy? Take a hot bath and relax? Walk in nature? What do you enjoy doing?

2. Tell people who care

Moira wanted to tell her mother about how down she had been feeling lately, but she didn't dare. Why? Her mother was the Queen of Denial. Everything to her mother was "high productivity and don't complain." Her mother denied her own sad feelings. Moira watched her mother zoom about keeping so busy that there was no time to experience a low mood. This led Moira to be uncomfortable about sharing her feelings with her mom, because it always appeared that her mom really didn't care. Worse, it made Moira feel bad for having sad feelings.

However, the truth is: We all feel sad sometimes—even crushed—and it really helps to have someone you trust listen to you.

If we tell the right person how we're feeling, the feeling now spoken often reduces in intensity. How? Unspoken fears or upsets rattle in our subconscious as BIG trouble stealing our personal energy.

But when you voice your trouble and even write it down, you made significant progress to "cut it down to size." Acknowledging the feelings you have make them easier to deal with.

Who do you know who will listen to you and give you some support? Do you need to find a counselor or therapist?

3. Expand from your "negative focus"

Here's a tough example. During the Holiday Season,

many people feel really low and troubled. Some may be facing the first Christmas-time without a romantic partner in many years. Others may be feeling "like an alien" when they see happy couples or happy families.

A powerful solution is to ask yourself energizing questions like: "Why am I starting to feel better?"

And then you can respond with:

- Because I still have four friends who care about me and I can set up times to get together over coffee.
- Because I still have a job (thank goodness!)
- Because I'm going to paint my picture today for 30 minutes.

At any given moment, we all have something bothering us. But we also have *Something Good* in our lives. Expand your focus so you can see the whole picture.

4. Pinpoint your purpose

He who has a why can endure any how – Friedrich Nietzsche

Researchers have observed how people with a purpose have extra resiliency. Even in a retirement home, an elderly person will live longer when they set a goal like: See my grandson graduate from college.

Pick your own "points of meaning." What do you value? What's important to you? Who is important to you?

What can you aim for—and look forward to?

It's not just about having one purpose like: Be a doctor or win the diving Gold Medal at the Olympics. You can take a purposeful approach to each day. You might focus on this idea: "I am kind to people I meet and I approach life with courage."

"If we don't stand for something, we'll fall for anything."
– Irene Dunne

Pick your purpose, and pick your values. Then support your values by taking action.

Don't judge each day by the harvest you reap but by the seeds that you plant. - Robert Louis Stevenson

You can raise your mood by going into purposeful action. Consider doing something for someone else.

Milton Erickson once cured an older woman of depression. How? He noted that she liked nurturing African Violets. What was the prescription that Erickson gave the woman? He said, "Raise the plants and give them to people at your church."

Soon many people were visiting the old woman and she had found a way to create more smiles among the people near her.

Her depression evaporated.

She now was truly connected to her community.

We all feel low at times. Do NOT stay there. Feel the sadness and find a way to use the S.T.E.P. methods.

You *can* feel better!

Make This Year Great for You: The TRUTH on How You Can Keep Going While Others Quit

The tension at the table in the restaurant felt like a smothering blanket. My former business associate looked at me with barely contained anger.

Things had not gone well. We had learned the hard way that we were not a match for working on a project together. The resulting impasse had cost months of paperwork.

I reached over for a napkin and my suit sleeve caught on my water glass. Then it was like time stopped for a moment. My water glass balanced on its edge then SPLASH—water spilled all over the table.

Amazing! That was just the thing to dispel the tension and the matter between us was ultimately resolved. It began with a suit sleeve and a glass of water.

When you are working on projects that are long term and mean so much to you, you're likely to meet with *resistance.* The Big Goals often include big obstacles and we need strategies to help us carry on.

A certain few people will make this year *great* for themselves. Many others will quit. But not YOU—when you apply the following strategies embodied in the N.E.W. process:

N - Nurture Levels of Goals

E - Energize through new ideas/skills

W - Work the Worst First cure to procrastination

1. Nurture Levels of Goals

Whether you keep going or quit depends on your skills to use your emotion to energize your continued progress.

By this I mean, your emotion, properly channeled, can help you endure and ultimately fulfill your Big Goal.

A lot of people quit when their positive feeling (like "Oh! I look forward to being 40 pounds lighter") fizzles out.

To really be sure to keep going, it helps to have multiple Levels of Goals.

I'm talking about *not* just relying on "positive motivation." Instead, use whatever works!

The solution is to have *multiple Levels of Goals.* We will start with the *Three Emotional Focus-Points:*

Three Emotional Focus-Points:

1) Golden Pull Goals

2) Dark Boot Goals

3) Green Tranquility Goals

Let's tackle the *Golden Pull Goal* (positive goal) of getting more sales. Sure, that is a positive thing. You might even make a plan to give yourself a personal reward when you accomplish more sales.

However, many of us realize that what really pushes us forward is a "Dark Boot Goal." It is like a boot that kicks us in the rear end. In this situation, a Dark Boot Goal would be "*avoid* having to tell my wife that the vacation is off because I failed to sell enough widgets." You work hard to make sure what you fear does NOT happen.

Along this line, here is another powerful "Dark Boot Goal": "*Avoid* tax penalties by turning in my tax return on time!"

Finally, after achieving many goals, I realized that I need goals that would *sustain* my well-being. I call these goals "*Green Tranquility Goals.*" I was inspired to use the word "green" upon hearing about a building that was built to be "green" and "self-sustaining."

We, human beings, need to be self-sustaining, too. For example, I schedule and take a walk every day and that is one of my Green Tranquility Goals. The walk helps me feel calm and peaceful.

So when you set a New Year's Goal, be sure to set up related Golden Pull Goal, Dark Boot Goal and Green Tranquility Goal.

2. Energize through new ideas/skills

You cannot solve a problem on the same level in which it was created. – Albert Einstein

When I was in my 20's I needed to raise funds to produce a feature film. I had no idea how to do it. For months, I suffered because I had a dream but also had big fears and no new skills. So what did I do? I gained a number of mentors and also began reading a lot. Now, I tend to read 80 books a year.

My focus is on getting new ideas and new skills each year because I do not know what new opportunities may arise.

With my clients and graduate students, I emphasize this idea: "You need preparation so that you're strong to face the unknowns."

To learn more about time management skills and ways to overcome procrastination, you can read my book *Nothing Can Stop You This Year*.

Here I'll now introduce you to the "Worst First cure" to procrastination . . .

3. Work the "Worst First cure" to procrastination

For many of us, procrastination is a habit. It is almost like a default setting. We feel that something may be unpleasant to do so we go on "automatic" and put it off.

Here is a better habit—an empowering habit: **"Worst First."** By this I mean do the worst task first. Here's an important observation: *The task you dread the most is the most important one for your career.*

If you're dreading updating your resume, it is probably the most important thing for you to do.

Personally, I dread doing paperwork. How do I handle it? I work on it first thing in the morning. Thirty minutes a day adds up when you do the Worst First task consistently.

Observe yourself. When do you have energy? When you wake up? Or later in the day? Or are you a night owl?

Some of my clients write from 5 pm – 6pm because they have a "second wind" at that time.

Use your best energy to apply to your Worst First task.

One college professor cleared his apartment of clutter by using the first 15 minutes of each day to clear clutter and straighten up.

Soon his living quarters were in great shape.

Now it's your turn.

What do you want to improve for this current year?

Identify your Worst First task and get going.

Make this current year *outstanding* for yourself.

Apply the N.E.W. process:

N - Nurture Levels of Goals

E - Energize through new ideas/skills

W - Work the "Worst First cure" to procrastination

You deserve to live the life of your dreams.

It begins today.

Believe in Yourself, Take Action–Do NOT Let Anyone Hold You Back!

"It's gotta get better than this!" I thought the first night I slept in an in-law apartment right next to Golden Gate Park, San Francisco. I slept on discarded chairs because I was afraid that the wild rats chasing each other in the walls would likely run over my body if I slept on the floor.

"Don't wish it was easier, wish you were better. Don't wish for less problems, wish for more skills." – Jim Rohn

The rat-infested in-law apartment (thanks to Golden Gate Park) was my experience many years ago. I'm so grateful that my life is better now. Now I will share skills and methods so you can make this current year *great* for you.

We will use the W.I.N. process:

W – Work your believing in yourself

I – Intensify emotion

N – Nurture your positive "Trigger Sequence"

1. Work your believing in yourself

Have you noticed how much is dumped on us against our

believing in ourselves? There are ill-advised parents and guardians who express negative opinions that hold many of us back. My father has done much of that *and I found a way out.*

The *problem* is that bad ideas from parents/guardians/former teachers are like weeds; they just grow on their own.

The *solution* is for you to work at pruning the garden of *your* mind.

To believe in yourself, work on two levels: the Conscious Level and the Subconscious Level.

a. Listen to your habitual thoughts and turn them around (work on the Conscious Level).

Habitual Negative Thought: "Oh. I'll screw this up. That's what Dad said."

Turn Around Thoughts: "I do NOT know that. My past does not equal my future.* I can do something different today. I can learn something better today."

* based on the quote "The past does not equal the future" from author Tony Robbins.

b. Impact your subconscious mind with positive messages daily.

Listen to positive audio programs. Devote time with people who believe in you (even if you need to hire a counselor/therapist/personal coach). Write down positive messages from people who build you up and repeat the positive comments to yourself each day—preferably *Out Loud.*

Set small goals and achieve small objectives. Your subconscious mind is watching you and how you make small, incremental improvements. Write down each small achievement. Researchers have discovered that a person needs to devote 10 seconds so that a positive thought takes root in the long term memory. Writing down your small achievement gives you those 10 seconds of focused attention. (I wrote about this in my book *10 Seconds to Wealth*.)

[As a side note: I share more details in my 7 minute video on YouTube, entitled "How to Believe In Yourself When Others Don't with Tom Marcoux."]

2. Intensify Emotion.

Emotion gets us in motion.

Many of us want to focus only on the positive. I agree that positive emotion can sustain you over the long journey.

My positive emotion about the value of my graphic novel series *Jack AngelSword* inspires me to make progress everyday.

At the same time, I'm aware of how some tough things in my life will improve when *Jack AngelSword* is serving many people.

You will get all you want in life, if you help enough other people get what they want. – Zig Ziglar

My point is: Intensify your emotion to move you so that you do the tough things that can really improve your life.

Use BOTH positive emotion and negative emotion. Many people are deeply motivated by "negative thoughts" like:

- I want the money to fix my teeth. If they get worse, I might lose the chance to get a new job.
- I want to stop living in this rat-infested building.
- I'll get the taxes paperwork done as fast as possible to avoid tax penalties.

Now it's your turn.

Tell yourself the truth as you ask yourself: What REALLY

gets me to take action? A positive goal? Or a big desire that something that's painful to me ends?

Use your strong emotional energy to make the current year better for you.

3. Nurture your positive "Trigger Sequence"

I will now share two Trigger Sequences faced by my clients.

- Martina comes home to an empty apartment after work. She feels lonely—and frankly bored. She sees the bag of tortilla chips on her coffee table. Her body knows something that will bring instant good feelings: tortilla chips and hot sauce. She reaches for the chips and eats. And she is not even hungry—for food. (She is really hungry for human connection.)

- Nadia wakes up in the morning and sees the binder of her weight loss book (that she is writing) —on her nightstand. Each day, she prints out pages in progress and places them in the binder. She realizes that she can apply an idea that arose in her recent dream to Chapter 3. She does not hesitate. She gets up 21 minutes early and types new words into a file of her upcoming book.

Trigger Sequences begin with a trigger. For Martina, the trigger is tortilla chips. That starts a negative Trigger Sequence.

For Nadia, the trigger is the binder of her weight loss book. Nadia's trigger begins a positive sequence of behaviors that yield her daily progress on her book.

To make this current year better, make sure you pay attention to your daily habits that include Trigger

Sequences.

Take care and transform your patterns (Trigger Sequences) so they support your highest good.

When you get strategic in your actions, you can BELIEVE that you will get big things done! Start small. Remember: Each little goal you complete builds *your* confidence in yourself that you can grow, change and get better. You create positive momentum.

* * *

Now, we will learn from Jeanna Gabellini's insights which help us "turn the corner" and approach each day with strength.

Pro or Amateur?
by Jeanna Gabellini

You have two choices in your business ... be a pro or be an amateur.

Professionals (pros) are people who take their hobby, sport or passion seriously. They've decided they're no longer satisfied with being an amateur. They want the challenge and fulfillment of fully living into their potential.

And when it comes to generating a FAT profit, you can't really get there by thinking like an amateur. If your business is treated like a hobby, it will be reflected in your bank account and your level of fulfillment.

If you want to increase your joy, confidence and make more money...go pro. Be a professional in your industry.

So how does a pro think?

You most definitely want to be very good at what you do. Unlike sports, business is not a competition, so you're not trying to kill yourself winning. **Pro is about being the best you can be, doing what you love as you enthusiastically pursue your wildest goals.**

You can't go pro if you don't dig what you do. Can you imagine trying to be a pro downhill skier if your passion is really soccer? No! You're investing energy, time and money to create your business...how can you stay committed through the finish line if you're doing something you don't love? You can't...so you have to really love what you've gotten yourself into.

Professionals...

- Can't wait to begin their work each day. Play and work have blurred lines.
- Get training they need, because they love expanding their skills. They like knowing what will enhance their experience or make them have an edge over what everyone else is doing.
- Hire the help they need because they know they can't do it alone. Think about NASCAR racers. While we celebrate the driver who wins...they couldn't win without their mechanics, car, coaching and sponsors. Every athlete has a coach or trainer. Everyone who has ever made it big had help.
- Study their performance to learn what they can do better. They get feedback from objective sources so they can improve their game.
- Don't dabble at their passion. They're either all in or not. Being a pro is a commitment. It requires the being-ness of someone who knows their power and wants to feel more of that connection through their craft or gift.

Amateurs...

- Don't expect much to happen so they hide and procrastinate.
- Don't create plans, structures, systems or practices to win. How can you follow through with glory when you don't plan to win?
- Try random strategies without thinking about the impact on their endgame.
- Are committed to their limited stories.
- Are easily distracted and it has NOTHING to do with ADD. They create pain for themselves.

Professionals can find themselves in these same habits but they recover quicker because their passion and desire to live fully calls them forth.

Everyday you have a choice...pro or amateur?

Seriously ... think about that choice. It's okay if you don't feel gung-ho about going pro right this moment. Maybe you need a confidence boost before you believe that you have what it takes to go pro (you do!).

Have a little chat with your Inner Business Expert and see what input you receive on this choice. Then make a decision ... Pro or Amateur? Whichever you choose, do it consciously rather than by default. Either way you'll be more empowered.

Going pro is an attitude, not about massive productivity. Pros work smart, not hard. When you're ready, put on The CEO/Pro hat. Everything becomes much easier and the results are ginormous.

"Going pro is FUN when I choose goals that get me fired up and work smart. I've got everything I need to run through the finish line."

Jeanna Gabellini is a Master Business Coach who

supports conscious entrepreneurs to double (and even triple) their profits by leveraging attraction principles, proven strategies and fun. She is also the co-author of *Life Lessons for Mastering the Law of Attraction*, with Eva Gregory, Mark Victor Hansen & Jack Canfield. And her book: *10 Minute Money Makers: How to Easily Double Your Profits in Just 10 Minutes a Day!* And her newest book, *Rock Your Profits!*

Combining vision, divine guidance and easy to implement actions, Jeanna delivers top-tier private coaching & sold-out seminars that have allowed committed entrepreneurs to blow past their self-imposed limits, ditch the drama of overwhelm and move into radical joy, inner peace and ever-increasing profits.

www.MasterPEACEcoaching.com

* * *

Now, Rebecca Morgan will guide us to a process in which we can change our behavior for the better and thus become stronger.

What Needs More Rigor in Your Life?
by Rebecca Morgan, CSP, CMC

Rigor is not a commonly used word nowadays. In this context, I mean diligence, precision, accuracy and meticulousness. The rigor I'm referring to means you are focusing on changing a behavior for the better. Typically starting or stopping a habit. Rigor takes extreme focus with a purpose.

For example, if you were trying to sharpen your golf game, you'd practice with awareness and consciousness, working to perfect your swing, stance or putt. You may engage a pro to help you refine your skills.

If you want to lose weight, you'll do better if you write down everything you eat and stay on a proven eating plan. You are more conscious of your hunger level instead of automatically reaching for a snack. You put in parameters that guide your behavior, like "no eating starches after 5:00," or "every day walk around the block upon rising." You may join a group program or hire a coach to help you stay on track.

Everyone has a habit or two that could use shoring up. Maybe you're always late to meetings, don't return emails for a few days, or forget to pack your lunch so you spend or eat more than you'd like in the cafeteria. You want to change the habit(s), but you don't seem to make much progress.

What could you do to add more rigor?

Tell another of your commitment. Having an accountability partner can be the motivation you need to shift behaviors.

Figure out what gets in your way of establishing the new behavior. If you're late because you don't notice the time, set an alarm. If you're a "one more thing" person, force yourself to just get up and leave in time. Put the tools in place to help you make the changes.

Track your results — daily (or perhaps hourly). You'll see your progress — or lack there of — and be more motivated to stay (or get) on target.

Commit to behaving consciously and purposefully around this change. Don't allow yourself to go on automatic. If you find you're slipping into the old behavior, stop and shift as soon as you're aware of it.

Changing habits isn't often easy. But if you add rigor to your desires, they will change more quickly.

Rebecca L. Morgan, CSP, CMC, specializes in creating

innovative solutions for customer service challenges. She's appeared on *60 Minutes, Oprah, the Wall Street Journal, National Public Radio* and *USA Today.* Rebecca is the bestselling author of 25 books, including *Calming Upset Customers* and *Professional Selling.* She is an exemplary resource who partners with you to accomplish high ROI on your strategic customer service projects. For information on her services, books, and resources, or for permission to repost or reprint this article, contact her at 408/998-7977,Rebecca@RebeccaMorgan.com, http://www.RebeccaMorgan.com/

* * *

Now, we will explore Randy Gage's thoughts about a mindset that will help you become stronger and enjoy life more.

Fear of Failure
A lightly edited transcript of a video episode
by Randy Gage

Hey guys, Randy Gage here.

Welcome to another episode of Prosperity TV. And I want to explore this issue of fear of failure because fear of failure can hold you back from doing something great. Something amazing. Something epic.

If you're thinking about how you might fail, what the ramifications may be, that may be the thing that stops you from doing what you're really capable of doing.

So let's explore that a little. Let's suppose that you're thinking about running a marathon and you don't make it. You make it 24 miles instead of 26.1 miles. Is that the worst thing that could happen?

You decide to climb Mt. Everest and you get four-fifths of the way there, and you have to turn around. And you don't make it to the summit. Is that really so horrific?

What if you really did get fired from your job? If I tried something new, if I take a chance, I could stand out. But maybe I'll fail!

Here's what I want to share with you. Getting fired was one of the best things that ever happened to me. Failing in a business is one of the greatest things that ever happened to me. Those things were course-corrections for me. They let me know that if I kept going on the path that I was going to go on, things weren't going to work out for my highest good. I look at them now as wake-up calls from the universe that let me know that there is a lesson for me to make this course-correction.

Then the greatest things in my life all came about after some of the worst things. So failure was not the worst thing.

I would just encourage you. Whatever you're afraid of, that you're thinking of something that you fear that you may fail . . . If you really did fail, what would be the worst thing that could happen? And then the question to ask is: *But what if you made it? What if you accomplished it?*

Until the next episode. Peace. I love you guys. And live rich.

Randy Gage is a thought-provoking critical thinker who will make you approach your business—and your life—in a whole new way. Randy is the author of nine books translated into 25 languages, including the *New York Times* bestseller, *Risky Is the New Safe*. He has spoken to more than 2 million people across more than 50 countries, and is a member of the Speakers Hall of Fame. When he is not prowling the podium or locked in his lonely writer's garret, you'll probably find him playing 3rd base for a softball team somewhere. He was born in Madison, Wisconsin.

www.RandyGage.com

Book Seven:
Put People at Ease: Feel Better through
50 Methods to Save 2 Hours a Day

A prime way of getting a new client is to set the person at ease.

When the client is with you, *you are* at ease and have "plenty of time" for the person.

How can *you* personally be at ease? Start with these *50 Methods to Save 2 Hours a Day.*

When you know and implement methods to improve your efficiency and effectiveness, you breathe easier. Better than time management, you will develop "time leadership." It is really about self-leadership. Let's begin:

The first Five Methods are grouped as the P.O.W.E.R. process:

P – Prepare Top Six Targets
O – Organize for momentum
W – Work the "Worst First"
E – Expand on paper
R – Recover (shake off rejection)

1) Prepare Top Six Targets

Many of us lose time in the morning because we do not have a good plan in the morning to jump right into action.

Here is a solution: Each night before I go to sleep, I take two minutes and write down my *Top Six Targets* for the next day. When I address an audience of businesspeople, I suggest: "Your Top Six Targets: two for you, two for family and two for work."

3) Organize for Momentum

To save time, be sure to pay attention to times when you have momentum and do not let people or things interfere. I call this plan both "organize for momentum" and "guard your momentum."

Some people find that they do well on a report or some other project and then tell themselves: "Oh, it's easier than I thought. I can take a break now." No! Stop! Keep going. Human beings get into a *state of flow* (as identified by researcher/author Mihaly Czikszentmihalyi) during which they function at their peak and they do not track time.

You can tell people: "I'm guarding my momentum."

You might say, "How about I give you a call ___[two hours later or the next afternoon]?"

Ask people: "Would you help me guard my momentum?" For example, my family knows that I am unlikely to appear for breakfast because from the moment I wake up I usually take on a "worst first" project or a writing project. I am fresh and strong in the morning so I want to use my prime energy to get the vital task done.

3) Work the "Worst First"

"Worst First" is a great habit to develop. You do what you dislike to do at the beginning of your workday. First, you're likely to have more energy so you'll do the task faster and in an efficient manner. You'll start your day with a personal victory. And, you'll save energy because you will not think of the task repeatedly through the day and suffer a loss of energy due to self-recriminations.

As I have shared with clients: **"You notice that THE thing that can most help your career is what you don't feel like doing."**

I have learned from the work of Dr. Kim McGonigal that

willpower is like a muscle. You are strongest in the morning but by the end of the day your "willpower muscle" is fatigued.

Save time and get more done by doing "worst first." You also save yourself from the energy most often lost to fretting over procrastination.

4) Expand on paper

Expand your perception by taking time to "think on paper."

Free floating anxiety drains energy and robs us of time and efficiency. Free-floating anxiety is defined as "a generalized, persistent, pervasive fear that is not attributable to any specific object, event, or source" (*Mosby's Medical Dictionary*).

When you think on paper, you dispel free floating anxiety. It's amazing. Any problem looks smaller once you reduce it to paper.

You can also save time by drawing on a piece of paper while you talk with someone.

For example, I drew three circles on a sheet paper when I was talking with my marketing team member. I said, "We're looking for the intersection. Some things a person is **Good at**, some things people will **Pay For**, and there are certain people you **Want as Clients."**

It was clear that the "intersection" was a small subset of the three different groups.

My team member understood my concept quickly because I drew the ideas on paper.

5) Recover (Shake Off Rejection)

We lose a lot of time if we allow an experience of rejection to throw off much of our day. To recover from rejection requires that we identify what personally works for us.

The truth is: Feeling rejected is often "an interpretation."

Instead of falling into a "they rejected me" trap, you can turn that around and tell yourself "We did not have a match."

For example, I was at a Chamber of Commerce gathering. Everyone in the room was there to do networking. I walked up to a group of three people. The central person said in a terrible tone, "This is a private conversation"—as if I did something wrong to approach the people for networking purposes.

Inside I felt like jumping somewhere to hide.

On the outside, I ad-libbed the response, "Oh. That's what I need to know." And I turned and walked away.

I took out a 3x5 card and *gave myself credit* for starting up another conversation. I kept with my plan to initiate ten conversations. Recognizing my courage and diligence to start conversations helped me feel better. That helped me to shake off feelings of being rejected. I reminded myself: "I only meet someone like that once in 200 meetings."

My next conversation was warm and friendly.

6) Write a Note to Find Your Place after an Interruption

Significant time is lost in trying to find your place in your work after an interrupting conversation has concluded. A number of office workers have found it helpful to say, "Just give me a moment." After jotting a note down, the person says, "I'm making a note as to where I am in this project. *Now* I can give you my full attention."

7) Do the "Two Minute Task" so it does not get on your "To-Do List"

At one point, a friend asked, "Tom, will you send me the

list of books I served as editor on?"

I replied, "I'm hanging up now. I'll pull that together and send it to you within the next 10 minutes."

My friend said, "Oh, you don't have to do it now."

"I do *not* want it to get on my to-do list," I insisted.

My point is: Do something quickly like place receipts from your purse or pocket into a folder. Do it now. Get it over with. Do not leave a bunch of unfinished little tasks lying around. Why? They drain you of energy. They are called "open loops." Instead, close a loop—that is, get the *Two Minute Task* done immediately.

8) Ask Questions (write a confirming email) to Avoid Miscommunications

Researchers have noted that an average of two hours are lost each day when people are untangling problem situations caused by miscommunications and misunderstandings.

Often with my interns and contractors, I write a confirmation email specifying actions and due dates while I am talking with the person. The team member then double checks the details and if all is in order replies with "got it."

If some detail is off, my team member revises my email message and then we set new parameters.

9) Double Your Energy by Clearly Seeing Your Progress

My phrase is: *Keep Score and Achieve More.* For example, as I type these words, I know that I am 44,118 words into writing this book. Researchers have identified a "speed up effect." As a person gets closer to completing a project—as she can see the finish line—she speeds up. You will become more productive and save time.

10) Set up a daily Self-Reward System

You cannot wait for the world to reward you. You need to reward your *consistent efforts* on a daily basis. How?

That's up to you.

My clients have provided themselves with

- A walk at lunch
- Reading a favorite novel
- Buy a new song from iTunes
- Having a spouse take care of the kids while the person has a relaxing hot bath and quiet time.

Rewarding yourself builds up your morale and increases your personal energy. With more energy, you get more done faster.

11) Set up daily Quiet Time/Meditation Time/Prayer Time

After directing feature films and writing twenty-six books, I have learned that accomplishing big projects does *not* bring total fulfillment. It is only *part* of a fulfilling, loving life. Long ago, my father said, "Do your duty." I replied, "I do my duty and it doesn't make me happy." This was the tip of the iceberg of something I realized. I needed another part of life. I identified this as "Green Tranquility Goals." The idea is that tranquility, feeling peace, and feeling loving and connected were vital parts of my life.

On a pragmatic level, after you have enjoyed some quiet time, you will return to your work refreshed and you will experience a new perspective. This state of being is ideal for creating and for moving forward with efficiency and effectiveness.

One thing that I find very helpful for experiencing tranquility and a sense of connection is music. One night, I was listening to the song "Learn to Love Yourself" sung by

Olivia Newton John. Her harmonies were breathtaking. I thought, "I'd like to fly to another state and see her live show." Then I realized that the experience of awe and feeling good were right here, right now. What brings you feelings of calm and tranquility? Add some form of quiet time to your daily life.

12) Keep a Clear Desk

Researchers suggest that we decrease our effectiveness by 40% when our mind jumps around to different projects scattered on our desks. For a number of people, it helps to clear the desk and *focus on one thing*. For those of us whose mind jumps around, consider having an Open File next to your work desk. *See the next method.*

13) Use an Open File Carton
(Avoid having to open a file cabinet)

An Open File is a set of files that you can quickly drop notes into. Researcher/Author Shawn Achor noted what he calls "The 20 Second Rule." He noticed that he just would not muster the energy to play his guitar because it took more than twenty seconds for him to go to the closet and retrieve his guitar from a closed guitar case. To solve this, he placed his guitar on a guitar stand and found that he played his guitar daily. The Open File Carton functions in the same way. You do NOT have to open a file drawer. You simply drop notes into the open files.

14) Stay fresh by changing work locations

J.K. Rowling did much of her writing of the first Harry Potter book at a family member's cafe.

I grade college papers on a train or in a car while a team member drives.

I write my books even in a notebook while waiting in line at Disneyland.

How can you change locations and energize yourself?

15) Use a dictation audio recorder

When I received the distribution agreement for my first feature film that I co-produced and directed, I pulled out an audio recorder and noted thirty-seven things I would NOT agree to.

Speaking into a dictation audio recorder speeds up the process for writing. Some people use the software Dragon for dictating emails, reports and other documents.

16) "Stand up" for energy

Change your physical positions throughout the day.

Stay in one position, and the body adapts and slows down. I was stunned that I actually fell asleep in the Mann's Chinese Theatre, Hollywood during an action scene. Just sitting in one place made it easy to fall asleep. If you feel "fuzzy headed" stand up, perhaps, even pace around a bit. Thomas Jefferson, Winston Churchill, Charles Dickens, Ernest Hemingway and Leonardo Da Vinci all had desks adjusted for them to stand and work simultaneously. A number of people say that standing provides a rest for their back.

17) Do NOT interrupt yourself

Research has demonstrated that human beings actually do *not* multi-task. Instead, a person has series of micro-stops and micro-starts. You stop looking at your computer screen for a fraction of a second to concentrate on your friend's voice on your telephone headset and then you stop again to look back at your computer screen. The person can tell that you're not fully present!

Instead, have a five minute conversation and then return your full attention to your work. You will save time and be more efficient.

18) Group Your Tasks

Many of us save time by doing all of our check writing or online bill paying at one time. Further, many of us do all of our errands that involve driving at one time.

19) Learn from "Reverse-Examples"

Pay attention to the mistakes people make. I listen carefully. Numerous people express complaints about their bosses. I listen to what is wrong and I fit that in with my studies of what good leaders do. Bad bosses are "Reverse-Examples" (They are *not* just sitting still; they are going backwards.)

I have also noticed how much disruption my father's habit of not listening to family members causes. He serves as a Reverse Example. And I have studied how to listen to people in better ways. Listening well actually avoids miscommunications and saves time.

20) Catch People Doing Something Right

One semester, the course scheduler sent me a proposed schedule for the upcoming semester.

I quickly noted that my classes were spread out over the week.

I wanted to encourage her to change the schedule so that I would enjoy having two classes on one day. That would reduce my overall travel time for the week.

Instead of pushing for my desire, I praised her for her kindness with the previous semester's schedule. I said,

"Thanks so much for doubling up two of my classes on Wednesday for this semester. It's worked so well."

The above is an example of "catching people doing something right." Poor communicators complain.

Good communicators praise. An old phrase is: What gets rewarded gets repeated.

21) During the day, "get off the stage"

You save time by doing things with lots of energy, focus and at a brisk pace. To do that, you need to recover your personal energy. How? Get off the stage. By this I mean step away from your desk and other people. Some people have a form of quiet time by walking down stairs between floors. Others take a break and listen to music in their parked car.

Do what you need to get a break from having to be "on" when you are in front of other people.

22) Get Your feelings to a "neutral place"

At one point in my life, I could feel my upset due to great stress swirl in my chest like a tornado. It was crucial for me to calm down or my upset could spread to my team whether we were on a feature film set or in the office working on graphic novel pages.

I have learned that it helps to have methods to get your feelings to a neutral place. Two things are important: 1) move effectively and 2) shift the direction of your thoughts. Both things can truly affect your feelings.

I don't sing because I'm happy; I'm happy because I sing.

– William James

Find out what are your "happiness triggers." Sometimes when I am working, I will listen to video of a performance by comedian Eddie Izzard.

Listening to Eddie Izzard's voice and humor shifts me

into a good mood.

Even if I am under stress, I can at least go to a "neutral place."

23) Create "Interrupts" for unresourceful-moods

When you feel a low mood rising up, you can "head it off at the pass." You can change the direction of your thoughts. One excellent resource is music. Some energizing music can shift a person's whole experience of the next moment.

24) Create ways to avoid following someone's bad mood

When I was in high school, we sat on the carpeted floor and waited for the next class. I did not know it at the time, but a football player who sat next to me was having a bad day. I did not know it until his fist hit me. (Fortunately, my karate training helped in this situation.) When I speak of "avoid following someone's bad mood," I am thinking: "Keep alert so you *notice* how other people are feeling." Secondly, use this principle: "Do not engage in mischief."

Pay attention and do something to "avoid engaging" with someone's bad mood. One method I use is to say "okay" with an upset family member. By "okay" I mean "I hear you." It does not necessarily mean "I agree."

If someone presses for agreement, I might reply: "I'll think about what you're saying."

25) Use your timer to allocate time for each task

Cyril Northcote Parkinson coined the phrase (known as Parkinson's Law): "Work expands so as to fill the time available for its completion." Do NOT let this happen to you. At various times during the day, I use a timer. It DOES improve my productivity. For example, earlier today, I said to my associate art director, "For a duration ten minutes, I want to go over some pages of *Jack AngelSword* and see if this outline is working." In those ten minutes, we confirmed the elements needed to be present in eight pages of the graphic novel.

26) Use an agenda for every meeting

Research shows that many professionals lose lots of time in meetings. When I worked in two banks, I was stunned and appalled at the amount of time wasted in meetings. With the assembled people, thousands of dollars per hour were devoted to the meeting (1 hour x 10 people).

Having an agenda and checking off details as the meeting goes helps create time savings.

Further, when you distribute the agenda before the meeting, people can be sure to bring the appropriate documents and do some critical thinking *before* the meeting. In the agenda, you can write "Come prepared to discuss and *set the criteria* for what will be an excellent solution to the XYZ problem."

27) Connect with "Desired Feelings" instead of just Goals

Researchers note that personal energy directly affects a person's productivity. I have learned that a Huge Reason connected to what you Want to Feel is an amazing source of energy. In my book, *Reduce Clutter, Enlarge Your Life*, I shared an example of how a husband got into action to eliminate a full, large storage locker—not for the money savings but for process of being able to fulfill his family member's dream to go to Avatarland (based on James Cameron's *AVATAR* feature film) set to open in 2017.

The husband's feelings were not tied to money. The feelings were about "seeing a family member's face light up with happiness."

Do you have something tough to do? Clear a garage, revise a resume, write and complete a novel? Tie into your powerful Desired Feelings. What, deep in your heart, do you want to feel?

28) Divide Goals into Effort-Goals and Result-Goals

The reason we divide goals between Effort-Goals and Result-Goals centers on keeping our personal energy and morale up and strong. In sales, an Effort-Goal can be "make thirty marketing calls this week." A related Result-Goal might be "gain three new clients." We notice: *You cannot get a Result-Goal without taking action on an Effort-Goal.*

You can be proud of yourself for your actions on Effort-Goals regardless of whether you meet a Result-Goal this week or next month. The truth is: Result-Goals are often based on things out of our control. The good news is that we *can control* our personal efforts toward Effort-Goals. When we do that, we feel better and our productivity soars.

29) Use the 4 M's for creating energy (Mind, Music, Movement, Meals)

Human beings are not machines, but we do *rely on our bodies to function well*—and to help us think well. It is best when we strategically take good care of ourselves through the 4 M's: Mind, Music, Movement, Meals.

For example, years ago, I discovered that eating a big hamburger had me feeling sluggish. I have avoided hamburgers for decades. This is an example of taking care with one's Meals.

Movement relates to exercise. "Mind" is about disciplining your thoughts. Some thoughts simply drain us of energy. Here is a terrible question: "Why does this always happen to me?" Instead, one can ask an empowering question: "How can we make this better?" or "How can I learn and improve my performance in this area?" Finally, it is best to pre-set a playlist of empowering music. It can get you moving faster and improve your productivity.

30) Plan what you will say—for maximum effectiveness

Author Lois P. Frankel emphasizes the value of "Headlines" and "taglines." Here is an example: One member of an association of townhouse owners wanted to convince her fellow owners that they needed to quickly cut down a tree to avoid it falling down on a neighbor's house.

At the meeting she gave this headline: "Now, I'd like to share with you three reasons why we need this tree cut down immediately." She then added a tagline, "After I share the three reasons, I'd like to open it up for discussion and hear your thoughts and feelings on this."

The headline tells people what your point is. The tagline shows that you are flexible and wish to respect others by listening to them.

The combination of headline and tagline makes it possible to gain cooperation faster.

31) Identify a person's "personal-pattern" and align your communication to it—and increase efficiency

I learned this "personal-pattern" distinction the hard way. Years ago, I asked an actress to come in to record new lines for her role in a feature film.

She replied, "No. I know what's going on. My acting coach said that when you record new audio lines, the editor only shows the back of your head. You lose close-ups." Her personal-pattern was completely self-centered. No appeal like: "If you do not record new lines, the feature film will not make sense. That hurts all of us" would help.

Today, confronted with that problem, I would state the problem only about how *she would* have a problem: "Your performance wasn't good enough. This is going to hurt you and your career. When you come in and fix the lines you won't have to worry about that. And you'll look good to other directors and casting directors. Your performance will reflect what a good actress you are."

Do you hear the difference? Her personal-pattern: total self-interest. My response: Frame the request for only her benefit.

It is important to speak in a way that aligns with the other person's "personal pattern." In essence, you express the facts in a way that is easily "digestible" to the other person. Thus, you gain cooperation.

32) Save time, get expert advice

My father wobbled precariously trying to ride a unicycle. He stretched his hand out to catch himself on a short wall at the boundary of a gas station. I said, "Dad, how about you hire a coach? In just twenty minutes, he or she will likely guide you and you'll be riding well." My father refused. He never got any coaching and ultimately discarded that unicycle.

This is NOT for you. Save your time. Seek coaching and insights of how you can do things more effectively.

33) Save time, become your *own* expert

One way to become your own expert is to log your results and write down your reflections about your results. I guide my clients to write down their results after a job interview. They write down "What worked" and "Areas to Improve." They harvest wisdom and plant seeds for improvement for the next job interview.

You can improve your performance faster by logging and reflecting on each time you step up to do something (a sales presentation, a speech, a job interview).

A note about experts: Sometimes "experts" cannot help you. You may be treading into new territory; certainly markets shift and change all of the time. Also, you are the person "on the ground." Finally, some "experts" are just good at reporting *what happened before.*

You may do much better by trusting your own intuition.

34) "Step out of the problem"

Albert Einstein said, "We cannot solve our problems with the same level of thinking that created them."

You need to expand your perspective. My favorite example is when Mark Burnett, creator of TV show *Survivor* needed to house his crew in a remote, tropical area. There were no appropriate facilities. Team members said the situation was impossible. Burnett said, "We *are* going to solve this." Eventually, the team came up with the solution: Rent a cruise ship and park it near the filming location. The cruise ship functioned like a floating city.

When you are faced with a problem, write it down on paper. Note the details (criteria) of what a good solution would look like. Then get lots of input from various directions. Consider blogs, websites and videos you do not normally visit. Perhaps, view documentaries on the History Channel and Science Channel to get varying points of view. Seek to combine existing ideas and form something new, if needed.

35) Choose energizing foods

Food can power you to be productive or food can slow

you down. Numerous nutritionists emphasize that a person needs fruits and vegetables rich in antioxidants including: kale, broccoli, collard greens, and spinach. I eat spinach for breakfast (early in the day is when my willpower is strongest). Eating healthy carbohydrates (particularly after an exercise session) is critical because they restore the body's glycogen stores. Researchers report that glycogen forms an energy reserve that can be quickly put into service. So to raise your productivity do some research into healthy eating.

36) Wake in Gratitude

Some people's first conscious thought in the morning creaks under the pressure of anxiety. Instead, condition yourself to wake up with a positive thought. Even write a couple of them down on a card, placed on your nightstand. As soon as you wake up, read the card out lout. My clients have chosen phrase like: "I'm grateful for this day for love, prosperity and happy surprises" and "Thank you, God for this day for joy and prosperity."

Why is "Wake in Gratitude" helpful to save your time? Many people (including me in my teenage years) wake up as if they are swimming through mud. They may not have something so enticing to get them out of bed quickly. If you hit the snooze alarm two times, you are probably losing twenty minutes easily.

Instead, condition yourself to focus on the positive and express gratitude out loud.

37) Sleep in trust

For people who have a spiritual practice, the method "Sleep in Trust" can help both in going to sleep faster and to sleep more soundly. You can have a card resting on your nightstand with some phrase like: "Thank you, God for a great refreshing sleep. I wake up feeling good and full of energy."

In essence, you are programming your subconscious mind.

To take this to another level, you can use Noah St. John's technique called an "afformation" which is a question that engages your mind in an empowering manner.

Here is an example:

"Why do I sleep well?" (the afformation).

Then the individual replies in their own mind:

"Because I'm safe. Higher Power wants me feeling good so I am energized to be good to people all day tomorrow."

38) Go for excellence, not perfection

"Life is about success, not perfection," wrote author Alan Weiss. This reminds me that it is vital to make good decisions and avoid losing time to perfect that which does *not* need to be perfect. What does *not* need to be perfect? Perhaps, a report that you know the team will revise in the next meeting.

Some people, known as control freaks, *lose a lot of time* making things look perfect even though the supervisor (if asked) would say, "That looks nice. But I don't care about that. Instead, we need you to do XYZ."

Pause before you start a project. Find out what is most important to do, and see if there is something that you can drop from the schedule.

Most people fail in life because they major in minor things.

– Tony Robbins

Instead, be sure to think clearly about what would make a project successful.

39) Eliminate time-wasters

You will face two terrible time-wasters in particular: a) those people who waste your time and b) your habits that waste your time.

For people who waste your time, you can say, "I can spare five minutes, then I have to [go to an appointment]."

In terms of your poor habits, you can change a pattern. For example, Shawn Achor, author of *The Happiness Advantage*, found that he was watching too much television. To change his habit, he set up a new pattern: he kept the batteries for the TV remote in a different room than the TV remote. In this way, it simply became inconvenient for him to watch television. He would work on his book or play the guitar because they were easier to access.

40) Use "completed staff work"

"Completed staff work" is a great way for a leader or manager to fully engage team members and reduce the leader's load. How? The leader says, "Do not come to me with a problem until you come up, on your own, with three alternative solutions. Then return to me. Tell me which solution you endorse and give me your reasoning." Completed staff work results in many people solving their own problem before they come back to the leader. The leader saves a lot of time.

I use this regularly. I often have an illustrator do two experimental sketches and then ask her to return to me, endorse one, and tell me the reasons for her preference. I often say, "Sounds good. We'll go with your recommendation."

41) Use binders and folders immediately

If the tools of organization slow you down, you are likely

to *not* use them. Instead, have empty binders, folders, pens, labels and all your tools for staying organized within easy reach. You will avoid having to go back and devote two hours to get organized. You stay organized by using binders and folders throughout your day.

42) Use "Easy Part Start" to create momentum

What is the easiest thing you could do to move a project forward? Write rough draft chapter titles? Do a Google search? Pick something that is easy and then transition into doing something tougher.

43) Use the Difference between "I want to do" and "I feel like doing"

Many of us get stuck and lose time when we proclaim to others statements like: "I hate filing" or "I don't want to fill out sales reports."

However, we can have a different perspective when we realize we *"want to fill* out a sales report to keep our job" but "I just don't *feel like* doing it." This distinction is more than semantics. It actually helps you key into what is most important to you. For example, you may not feel like doing your tax return but you do WANT to avoid tax penalties. So you will likely take action to protect yourself.

44) Power up Your Personal Brand

When people know your positive personal brand, they trust you and cooperate sooner. This saves you significant time. Your personal brand is the answer to the question: "What are you best known for?" It is also a promise of performance. People trust you to come through. I guide my clients to develop a positive personal brand based on "T.H.O.R."—which stands for Trustworthy, Helpful,

Organized, and Respectful.

45) Use the "slice the pizza" method

An old phrase is: "Inch by inch, it's a cinch. Yard by yard, it's hard." One way to increase your productivity is to slice a big task into smaller pieces. Set up a series of deadlines. Begin with easy parts and then you will begin to feel the momentum. This reminds me of the old phrase: "How do you eat an elephant?—one bite at a time."

46) Save time by hiring a coach

When a number of people go into a new industry they flail about, experimenting for months or years. When I began in the speaking industry, I immediately hired a coach for two hours. Through her guidance, I made money immediately by producing products for purchase at my presentations. Hiring a coach can help you leap forward!

47) Save time by hiring assistance by the project or by the hour

I have learned that I can save 2.5 hours by hiring an assistant for one hour. How? I get things done before the assistant arrives so that the one hour I am paying for is utilized efficiently. Also, I find that I am "fired up" after the one hour is done. So I keep going at a faster pace than I would usually.

48) Save time by reading (or listening to audio books)

Recently, one of my friends faced a dilemma involving a particular business. I woke up the next morning and my subconscious mind served up a number of new ideas that my friend might find useful. I called my friend and shared the insights.

Having a lot of ideas can help you land on the good ones which help you save time and get great results.

A few hours after my conversation with my friend, a family member asked about my reading 81 books a year. I replied, "I am conditioning my mind to think of different ideas and to combine the findings of many learned people." For example, when I innovated the idea of Personaltainment Branding (found in my book *Yes! Secrets for Your Best Life*), I combined observations of a number of people including Bill Gates, Tony Robbins, Seth Godin and others. I was aware of their observations and insights by reading a number of books.

Be sure to have a lot of positive, insightful, and useful input: Read books or listen to audiobooks.

49) Save time by using a timer for certain phone calls

In 1988, a *New York Times* article reported that top Hollywood mogul Jeffrey Katzenberg made around 600 phone calls a week. He was called "the master of the 2 minute phone call." Katzenberg had two secretaries who split the Katzenberg day between them. You see they placed the calls and had people hold so that Katzenberg could talk to people on the phone in turn.

At one point, I had a particular friend who would engage in long phone conversations with me. To cut down on the time, I would set a timer for 10 minutes. When the timer would chime, I would invite us to double check if we wanted to continue or bid each other, "Talk to you later."

For some long-winded people, you can say, "I'm about to head into an appointment. I can talk for 10 minutes at most." You are saying an appointment—and that can mean *an appointment with yourself* to do something crucial to improve your career.

50) Start the morning with something that "pulls you"

Earlier I mentioned Wake in Gratitude so that you have positive energy in the morning. Additionally, pick something that you want to do—and that you feel like doing—so that you jump out of the bed quickly. Often, I wake thinking of details for a book I am writing. So I get up and immediately start writing. It feels good to capture the good ideas from my subconscious mind. Other people begin their day by listening to empowering music or reading from a supportive, spiritual text.

* * *

Again, I emphasize that the powerful way to set the other person at ease is to be at ease yourself. The other person feels better when he or she feels that you have "plenty of time" for him or her.

When you implement even one of the above *50 Secrets to Save 2 Hours*, you feel calmer and better. You know that you are lightening your own load. You have set forth on a better path and a welcoming smile easily graces your face.

In essence, becoming skilled with time helps you in your journey of making a great first impression with anyone you meet.

Book Eight:
Your Advantage –
The Training Section for
Making a Great First Impression
and Power Networking

For my clients and students, I developed a training system titled **"The *Communicate to Win* Advantage."**

Here I will function as your coach by addressing fifty questions and providing answers. After each answer, I then ask *you* specific questions so you can develop your own Action Plan.

(I suggest you write your answers either in this book or in a personal journal. Even devoting 20 seconds to writing your personal answer to a question will help you gain more benefit than merely reading this section of this book.)

Let's begin:

Communicate to Win

Question #1: What is the benefit from studying and practicing communication skills?

Answer: Powerful communicators experience a most delicious and unexpected pleasure. The unexpected pleasure can be a raise, more closeness with a romantic partner and/or other positive outcomes. And in particular, we're talking about making a great first impression.

Question #2: What are the Five Factors of Influencing people?

Answer:

The Five Factors of Influencing People

1) Show how much you care

179

2) Show how you have common traits, concerns and feelings

3) Show how much they will personally profit from taking action

4) Show how you are a trusted, credible advisor

5) Approach people in the way they prefer (based on personality styles and input styles)

Write down your answers to these questions:

1) How can you show how much you care?

2) How can you show how you have common traits, concerns and feelings (with the person)?

3) How can you show how much he or she will personally profit from taking action?

4) How can you show how that you are a trusted, credible advisor?

5) How can you approach people in the way they prefer (based on personality styles and input styles)?

[**A brief discussion about personality styles.** According to research and anecdotal evidence, we note that people have these personality styles:

a) Director (label: Lion)

A person who is hard-charging and bottom-line orientated. *(Approach: Be brief and facts-orientated.)*

b) Relater (label: Dog)

Someone who is most concerned with how people are affected. Someone who is loyal and relationship-focused. This person likes routine. *(Approach: Be warm and listen a lot to this person.)*

c) Socializer (label: Peacock)

A person known as the life of the party. Someone who likes ideas and to be the center of attention. Like a peacock, they like to show off. *(Approach: Demonstrate that you like this person and let them be the center of attention. You do the follow-up call to this person.)*

d) Analytic (label: Beaver)

Frequently, this person is an accountant or engineer (hence the reference to "builder of dams.") A person who prefers charts, tables, graphs, and "all the data." Often this person is slow to make a decision. *(Approach: Be thorough and provide data and evidence.)*]

[**A brief discussion about input styles.** People tend to respond more to a particular mode of input: Visual, Auditory or Kinesthetic (body/touch/feelings based).

a. Visual. You can recognize this person in that they often say, "I **see** what you're talking about. It **looked** good to me." *(Approach: Show the person a brochure, a photo, a video or something else.)*

b. Auditory. You can recognize this person in that they often say, "I **hear** what you're saying. It **sounds** good to me." *(Approach: Talk slower. Lower the pitch of your voice so that it is pleasing to the ear. Provide something that sounds good: music, a video with a narrator who has a good voice.)*

b. Kinesthetic. You can recognize this person in that they often say, "It didn't **feel** right to me. [or] The meeting went **smoothly.** [or] I think you'll be a **good fit** for the team." *(Approach: Allow the person to "prove it to herself." Provide a calculator so she can calculate the savings herself. Make the situations comfortable—for example, give the person a comfortable chair.)*

Section 1: Communication Quick Tips
Personal Help
Win the Life of Your Dreams

Question #3: How can you come across (in a first meeting) as someone who is at ease and who is positive about life?

Answer: Learn to create steady progress in your own life and *your good feelings will naturally radiate* from you. Because of *mirror neurons* (brain cells in the other person that reflect what they pick up from you), you want to "broadcast" your own feelings of ease.

We create steady progress by using what I call *Emotional Self-Leverage,* which is a science I have developed over the years. It is based on human motivation and reactions. It focuses on helping you gain leverage on yourself so you accomplish a task that will improve your life. You cast off procrastination.

In Emotional Self-Leverage, we notice two forces: a) the *positive* that pulls you forward—like a dream; and b) the *negative* that pushes your forward to avoid something painful (like a tax penalty). In your daily life, you use Emotional Self-Leverage by linking a "pull" or "push" to your task.

Write down your answers to these questions:

1) How can you use the *Positive* (the pull)? (examples: a reward that you give yourself; listening to your favorite music while exercising)

2) How can you use the Negative (the push)? (Example: enlist a friend to monitor your exercise schedule and to penalize you [some monetary amount] for each day you fail to exercise. Have the money go to a charity.)

Win Wealth, Abundance and Prosperity
Question #4: What is a key to wealth?

Answer: A key to wealth is a spiritual phrase: "I am here only to be truly helpful." Discover how you can help people on a massive level, and you create your stream of wealth.

Here are three methods to be truly helpful:

    a) (For those on a spiritual path) Ask for Higher Power's guidance in the moment

    b) Stay aware that truly helpful actions vary, depending on the situation

    c) Ask the other person what he or she prefers you do to help.

Write down your responses:

1)   (For those on a spiritual path) Note a prayer for asking for Higher Power's guidance in the moment

2)   Note different ways you can ask the other person what he or she prefers you do to help. (Example: "How can I be supportive of what you're doing?"*)

3)   Identify something you need to learn (and you might apply your new knowledge as something you can teach others).

* When it comes to developing positive relationships, asking "How can I be supportive of what you doing?" can be helpful. Another valuable question is: "How could I recognize if someone is a good client for you?"

Win Wealth, Abundance and Prosperity

Question #5: What is a key to getting someone to buy your product or engage your service?

Answer: The key is the other person's feelings.

Here are two principles to keep in mind:

a) "People buy on emotion and later justify on fact.

b) "People like to buy, but they do NOT like to be sold."

Write down your responses:

1) Write down three questions that can help the person express how they want to feel upon buying your product. (Example: How would you personally benefit if this solution was in place? How would that feel to you?)

2) Write down three ways that you might come across as pushy or as selling hard when you talk to a potential client. How can you modify your approach and help the person discover how they will enjoy benefits of your product?

Win at Love

Question #6: What is a key toward enhancing love*?

Answer: Inquire about the person's values and "sparks." A *value* is something that is most important to the other person. Think of a value as the "flame." A *"spark"* is how the person wants something to be.

1) To discover the person's value, ask, "What is most important to you in a loving partner?" Use this question "In order for you to feel close, what do you need from me?" Or write a different version of this question.

2) To discover, the "spark", use this question: "In order for you to feel that I love you, what do you need me to do?" Or write a different version of this question.

* People who take good care of their personal relationships feel at ease in their daily life. This will help when you wish to make a

great first impression in your business life.

Win by Creating Better Relationships

Question #7: How do you create a positive relationship—from the start?

Answer: Ask "gentle questions" and find a way to be helpful to the person.

A gentle question is one that is easy and often fun for the person to answer.

Ask questions like:

1) What are you looking forward to?

2) Who is your ideal client?

3) How would I recognize someone is an ideal client for you?

4) What are the trends in your industry?

5) How can I be supportive of what you're doing?

6) What is one of your hobbies?

Win by Overcoming Fear

Question #8: What is a good way to overcome fear of meeting people?

Answer: Preplan your responses and rehearse your responses. With my clients, I share the image of a kind grandmother saying: "Feeling fear? Rehearse my dear."

I emphasize: "Courage is easier when you're prepared."

Write your answers to these questions:

1) What tough situation do you have coming up?

2) What could go wrong or be troublesome?

3) What could you say/do in response to the situation?

4) What else could you say/do in response to the situation?

5) Where can you get more information about making

effective responses?

6) Is there something you can rehearse with a friend or a coach?

Win by Overcoming Procrastination and Show Your Trustworthiness

Question #9: How can you get people to trust you faster?

Answer: Demonstrate that you do *not* procrastinate. For example, I was talking with someone who has edited eight books (of 26 books) that I have written. He asked that I send a list of the books. I said, "I'll hang up now and email the list to you in about 10 minutes."

"You don't have to do it now," he said.

"I do not want this task to even get on my to-do list," I replied.

My point is: If people see you get to work quickly and that you do not procrastinate, you become extraordinary (and trustworthy) in their eyes. Why? Because, I have noticed, a lot of people procrastinate. Even worse, a lot of people promise to do something and then fail to do it!

Here's another example: When you meet someone new, put an envelope with a hand-written note into the mail immediately after the meeting. How do you do that? You have envelopes half-done (your handwritten return address and a stamp on the envelope) prior to the networking event. Then after the event, hand-write the person's address on the envelope. Then hand-write a note. Author Bob Burg suggests that you write these words: "Hi Dave (or Mary), thank you. It was a pleasure meeting you. If I can ever refer business your way, I certainly will."

Write Your Responses:

1) Will you prepare hand-written follow-up notes

(and stamped envelopes) to use in your
networking efforts?

2) Will you develop strategies to overcome
procrastination?

For example, I use the process "Worst First." I tackle a
tough task early in the day. Why? Dr. Kelly McGonigal,
author of *The Willpower Instinct,* cites research that our
willpower is like a muscle that becomes fatigued later in the
day. It is best to tackle tough tasks when we're fresh.

Secondly, when I start a tough project and I achieve some
momentum, I stick with it. I know that I can get more done if
I get in a solid 30, 40 or 55 minutes on the project.

Thirdly, I do some work on a long project every day. I
keep a Progress Log to record my getting in my daily 30
minutes on a particular project.

Win by Increasing Your Confidence

Question #10: What is a good way to increase my
confidence?

Answer: Start easy. It helps when you realize that
confidence really comes from a certainty in yourself that you
will learn what you need to and that you will not stop until
you succeed. With my clients, I share the basis of real
confidence "A.L.F." – Adapt, Learn, Flex (as in being
flexible).

Write your responses to the following items:

1) What task gives you feelings of
nervousness?
2) What do you need to learn?
3) Where can you get training or coaching*
4) If you feel nervous about meeting new
people, write down some appropriate words
you can express when beginning a

conversation.

5) Note what warm colors work for your wardrobe. Looking good can support your confidence.

* Consider contacting my office via tomsupercoach@gmail.com for a variety of resources including coaching in-person or on the telephone—or special video training programs.

Win by Making a Great First Impression
Question #11: How do I make a great first impression?

Answer: Interview the person and only "sprinkle" items about yourself.

Write your responses to these details:
1)   How will you dress like a trusted advisor?
2)   Prepare some gentle "interview" questions like:
- How do you know our host, Mark?
- What do you like about these Chamber of Commerce events?

3)   Write down a couple of positive details about yourself that you can "sprinkle" into your conversation like:
- Oh—I am looking forward to my first book coming out in October. Do you prefer to read books or see videos when you're looking for information?
- [Responding to a compliment about music notes on one's tie] Yes, it reminds me of the times when I compose songs. Do you have a favorite singer or movie soundtrack composer?

Win through Humor
Question #12: How do I improve my sense of humor and start to use humor?

Answer: Expose yourself to more humor forms. Watch funny home videos, see standup comedians (avoid their put-downs and offensive language). Learn the structure of humor (to learn more about humor see my book *10 Seconds to Wealth*).

Author/Speaker Roger Dawson notes Five Forms of Humor: Exaggeration, Puns, Putdowns (avoid these), Silliness and Surprise.

For your own humorous stories . . .

Exaggeration: ("I shoveled snow with a shovel as big as a toothpick.")

Puns (example: the agony of the feet – "defeat")

Put-downs (only use self-deprecating humor. Author Denis Waitley talks about the folly of his youth: As a young man he wore his fighter pilot flight suit while mowing the law — so his neighbors would know who lived next door!)

Silliness (pick your own example)

Surprise (often the surprising twist is what makes something funny. For example, the classic Henny Youngman line: "Take my wife – please!" has a twist.)

Win when Pushing Against Policy

Question #13: What is a key to getting what I want when dealing with policy?

Answer: The primary technique is to go up the chain of command. As you continue to do business, it is good to develop a personal brand that appears as "firm but fair." People who are strong and speak up for what they want in a calm, consistent manner often receive respectful responses.

So when you request to "talk with the manager," use a calm, polite and clear approach.

Clerks can only implement policy; they are not empowered to step beyond policy. For that, you need to go to a manager, supervisor, vice-president or above. If the situation is crucial, start at the top. Call the CEO, and the administrative assistant will probably send you to another office. AND, you now have the leverage of saying "CEO Janet Goroson's office sent me to you about..."

1) Say, "Please pass me to someone at their level or above." Use a question like: "Who can help me get satisfaction today?"

2) Speak the Language of the Company. What are their buzzwords?

3) Establish your credibility. State a relevant credit of yours ("I write for a consumer e-newsletter....")

4) Zero-in on de-escalating language. (Instead of "I want my money back," use "We just need to make a little adjustment.")

Career Help
Win a Job

Question #14: When and how do I talk about salary in a job interview?

Answer: Leave the salary discussion for last if possible. You need to *first* prove that you're going to be a major asset to the team.

1. Use Effective Responses to an Early Question of "What are your salary requirements?"

a) "Oh, are you offering me the job?" [Usually, the person will back down and say, "Oh—not yet. We need to talk some more."

b) "My salary requirements are in line with current market rates for someone with my skills and experience. I'm hoping we'll continue talking about how I'll help the team to ..."

2. Prepare for the Usual Questions that include:

a) I see a gap in your resume. What were you doing then?

b) Why did you leave your last position?

c) What do you want to be doing in five years?

d) Describe your ideal job.

e) Why do specifically want to work here?

3. Prepare Your Own Questions:

a) In order for you to know someone is an ideal candidate for this position, what has to happen?

b) (A variation) In order for you to know someone is a match for this job, what has to happen?

c) What's most important to you in the ideal candidate for this position?

Win over Stress, Conflict and Change in the Workplace

Question #15: What is crucial to know about stress and conflict in the workplace?

Answer: You need to do two things: become stronger and communicate powerfully.

Become Stronger

Focus on this question: "Is there a way for me to take better care of myself now?" Note your answers and use your calendar to schedule taking action on your answers.

How can you "get off the stage"?

(Examples: take a break, take a walk, listen to music in your parked car)

Communicate Powerfully

Question #15a: How can I get along better with co-workers?

Answer: Build a positive "emotional bank account" with

each person. The emotional bank account is like a reserve of feelings that are between you and the person. If you fulfill a promise, you make a deposit in the emotional bank account. If you embarrass the other person, you have made a withdrawal from the emotional bank account.

What sincere compliments can you say to the person?

What promises have you made and how can you be supportive of the other person?

What gestures of appreciation can you give to the person? (Examples: thank you card, small box of chocolate, small actions that are supportive.)

Win a Raise/Promotion

Question #16: How do I earn a raise or promotion?

Answer: Ask the decision-maker, "What is most important to you—so that by the next review I have earned a raise (or promotion)?"

Go into the meeting with documentation:

a) Letters/email from happy customers

b) Notes/email from the supervisor patting you on the back

c) Your desk calendar with all overtime (if appropriate) logged and other notes, etc.

d) Training and education

e) Notes of how you made money, saved money, or saved time for someone to make money for the company

f) Some things that you did (notes taken at the time) that became company policy

g) Various email praising your performance

Win Your Way in Meetings

Question #17: How can we save time in meetings (and

make a good impression as a leader)?

Answer: Write down the following details:

What are elements for your agenda?

Who can be a good facilitator (one who makes sure that people participate)?"

Who can be a good recorder (one who writes down the ideas of the group—on a large sheet of paper)?

What decisions need to be made?

What are ideas for the *criteria of a good decision*? (Perhaps there are constraints like hours, number of team members, budget.)

Track Effort-Goals (daily tasks like 10 marketing phone calls) and Result-Goals (5 new clients per week)

Win More Productivity from Your Team

Question #18: How can I lead my team to more productivity?

Answer: Use a system to reward those who achieve Effort-Goals (daily tasks like 10 marketing phone calls) and Result-Goals (results like gain 5 clients per week).

What Effort-Goals do you want to set with your team?

What Result-Goals do you want to set with your team?

How can you post results of people achieving Effort-Goals? (A chart, a line-graph, "30 days accident free.")

Use emotional "word pictures" to move people to action (Example: "It's like a person on a life raft—in the ocean—flowing into a commercial lane. Now, he is likely to be seen.")

Show your team members how each person individually profits from positive outcomes.

Win Sales

Question #19: What is the key to sales?

Answer: The key is using the process of asking questions, listening and only talking about what's important to the prospective client.

What questions can you ask your prospect so that your responses only address the prospect's concerns?

What can you offer that creates *Customer Delight* (something that is extra and surprising)?

How can you begin by giving something first (a free report, an ebook, or something else)?

Write in your journal:

a) Your goals

b) Some form of a *tracking system* (for example: you could track how many marketing phone calls lead to an in-person meeting and how many meetings lead to a sale).

Win when Deal-Making and Negotiating

Question #20: How can I become stronger when negotiating?

Answer: Use the *Principles of Influence* as developed by author Robert Cialdini.

1) Reciprocity
2) Commitment and consistency
3) Social proof
4) Authority
5) Perception of scarcity
6) Liking

1) How can you create the feeling in the person that he or she needs to reciprocate (give something back)? (Reciprocity)

2) How can you get the person to commit to something small? (Commitment and consistency)

3) How can you show that the product provides real benefits for other people? (Social proof)

4) How can you demonstrate that you are a trusted advisor? (Authority)

5) How can you give people the perception that there is a limited amount of what you are offering? (Perception of scarcity)

6) How can you guide people to like you? (Liking . . . example: Do more listening.)

Business Help
Win with the Telephone

Question #21: How can I be more persuasive on the telephone?

Answer: Preplan your call.

Preplan your call:
1. Personal referral
2. Express a benefit (example: "Double your sales")
3. Ask, "Is this a good time to talk?"

How can you gain a personal referral?

How can you express a benefit?

Will you ask "Is this a good time to talk"? Or will you modify the question?

Bonus Tip: Use a mirror to help you ensure that you smile.

Win with a Web Site (Blog) and E-commerce Advantage Strategies

Question #22: What's most important to remember when creating and using a website?

Answer: Give something and create your own "tribe."

A tribe is a group of people connected to one another, connected to a leader, and connected to an idea.... A group needs only two things to be a tribe: a shared interest and a way to communicate.

– Seth Godin

One of my clients asked, "So I need a website?" I replied, "Not a website. A blog would be better. Then you can create your tribe. Also you can 'blog your book.' After one year of weekly blog posts, you have the material for a book." She did just that. And with my guidance, after a year, she had a book manuscript and book proposal that convinced a top publishing company's senior acquisitions editor to take her book to the committee. (Alas, the book died in committee because committee members said, "We already have a number of books 'for beginners.'")

Here is the good news. She went from zero to blog visitors from 141 countries.

She now has 3 books that sell every month.

What do you have a strong interest in?

Where is your expertise?

Will you be able to write with passion about your topic each week? Or will you be able to have guest posts from guest authors?

Can you make the topic really focused? (An old phrase is "Grow rich in a niche." For example, it is said that 40% of the population are introverts. If you are an introvert, think of what you really need to improve in your own life. Think of your own fears and aspirations.)

What can you offer for free? Of course, you have free blog posts. How about videos? Would you like your own YouTube channel?

Consider having your own e-newsletter. Think of what you can offer that is different than what you usually provide in blog posts. Will you provide information that goes deeper into your topic? Will you provide links to your exclusive videos?

Win by Speaking before Groups

Question #23: How do I handle my fear of speaking before groups?

Answer: Four methods in particular help with dealing with the fear of public speaking. We'll use the R.E.A.L. process:

R - Rehearse

E – Engage a coach

A – Align with "Recovery Methods"

L – Learn as you go

1. Rehearse

I emphasize with my clients whom I guide to be better public speakers: "Picture a kind grandmother who says, 'Feeling fear? Rehearse my dear.'"

Consider rehearsing for 9 minutes a day for 7 days instead of a block of rehearsal (one session of 63 minutes). Why is this preferable? Because your nine minute session will jump start your subconscious mind to work on your speech throughout your day. (You can also rehearse material that you will say when meeting people at a networking event. Your subconscious mind will work on your presentation in the background for seven days!)

2. Engage a coach

At the beginning of my speaking career, I immediately hired a coach for two hours. She set me on course and I began immediately to earn income through speaking.

Working with a client, I can pinpoint something that can

be adjusted. I can also provide a tried and true method.

For example, some people unconsciously rub their hands together. If someone says, "I'm confident that my product will solve your XYZ problem," but her hands are rubbing each other, then her behavior speaks louder than her words.

I am able to guide the nervous speaker to place her hands so that she *looks confident*.

My expertise comes from experience on the platform, and I have been a professional speaker and member of the National Speakers Association for 14 years.

I coach from my experiences and guidance from my own mentors.

I remember that my father wanted to learn to ride a unicycle. I suggested that he hire a coach for 20 minutes. He never did. He tried riding that unicycle, failed and disposed of the unicycle.

This is NOT for you.

Consider engaging a coach.

3. Align with "Recovery Methods"

I teach Recovery Methods as one of the first processes in guiding a client who wishes to be a better public speaker. I emphasize "align with Recovery Methods" in that many people get stuck and fall "out of alignment with the audience."

When you use a Recovery Method, you avoid breaking your stride. You stay connected and aligned with your audience.

My students say that their big fear is "getting stuck and having my mind go blank."

I guide my students to use Recovery Methods including:
- Take a drink of water.
- Say, "I'll need to pause for a moment. I want my

answer to be valuable for you."

- Say, "I haven't looked at it quite that way before. I'll need to pause for a moment. I want my answer to be useful to you."

When you have rehearsed Recovery Methods, your fear quiets down because you know you're ready for "bumps in the road."

4. Learn as you go

One way to do well with speaking is to take a "gradual, level-by-level" approach. You can begin by speaking and rehearsing in front of four supportive friends. Consider joining Toastmasters, where you will get the support of other speakers who are refining their communication skills.

* A Special Note: If you speak at an association meeting, suddenly you have a higher status than as a peer. You now have gained "expert status" and people will look to you as having more knowledge and credibility. In essence, you make a *Great* first impression!

Win at Making a Brand

Question #24: How do you make a brand name?
Answer: We will use the N.O.W. process:

N – Nurture a story
O – Organize your Unique Selling Proposition
W – Work to be trusted

1. Nurture a story

People remember a story better than a list of benefits. For example, a Walt Disney World "cast member" (employee) told a little girl that she could not bring an ice cream cone on an attraction. He said, "I'll hold it for you."

When the little girl and her parents returned, the cast

member was holding the ice cream cone. The parents knew that the cast member had just returned with a new ice cream cone because the original one would have melted in the hot Florida sun. Now, that's service!

To really build your brand, organize the good details that you do into a series of stories.

For example, when I want to get a new client to feel how effective my techniques are, I often tell a story of how my methods helped one of clients secure an internship with Donna Karan International in New York City. And now that person has a full-time job with Donna Karan.

Write your responses to the questions in this section in your journal.

What are three of the best benefits you provide customers? Now, identify two stories per benefit. That is, have two stories that are memorable and help the listener feel the benefit you are mentioning.

2. Organize your Unique Selling Proposition

What makes you stand out from the competition? Here is an example: "Domino's Pizza: Fresh, hot pizza to your door in 30 minutes or less. Guaranteed." That Unique Selling Proposition helped Domino's break in and dominate the glutted pizza industry. [Domino's later dropped that U.S.P. when some of their drivers had accidents.]

Years ago, I went to a particular photographer, Allen, to have my headshot done (the photograph that an actor or speaker uses in publicity materials). At times, I have a tendency to smile too big. So I intended to only have a small smile. But then Allen made me feel so comfortable and got me to have a genuine smile and CLICK, he captured it. So a Unique Selling Proposition that Allen could have used is: "I'll make you so comfortable that I'll capture a photo in the instant you look your best!"

Write down three rough drafts of a possible Unique Selling Proposition that you can use.

3. Work to be trusted

A huge element of a brand is that the customer trusts that you will deliver certain elements consistently. At the time of this writing, I went to see the Walt Disney Animation studio feature film, *Big Hero 6*. I had never heard of the Marvel Comics series entitled "Big Hero 6" until I heard that a new Disney animated feature film was soon to hit theaters with that title.

With Walt Disney Animation, I trust that the film will be fun, inspire laugher and include heartwarming moments. Seeing *Big Hero 6* in the movie theater delivered all three elements. I even cried two times to the heartfelt moments.

What elements do you want customers to know that you deliver consistently?

Section 2: You Deserve to Feel Happy

This book is about making a great first impression. If you come across as generally happy, then your potential client or friend does not interpret your behavior as that of a "needy person."

Take Care of Yourself
Replace Fear with Love

A number of spiritual paths emphasize that love can serve to overcome fear. The idea is that, in any given moment, one can be in a positive state "love," or in a negative state "fear."

Question #25: How does the process of replacing fear with love connect with making a great first impression and communicating well?

Answer: The salesperson who is afraid that he won't make this month's quota may radiate his fear. This will get the prospect feeling uncomfortable and he or she may not even know the reason.

The idea is for the salesperson to shift to a present-moment focus on serving and helping the person in front of him.

I often describe this as shifting from "How am I doing?" to "How are YOU doing?" My example is how I was terrified (at nine years old) of making a mistake while playing piano for 31 seniors at a retirement home. Now, years later, my focus, as a speaker, is about serving the audience. It is not "How am I doing?!"; it's about "How can I be focused on *your* concerns and *your* best interests?"

One time an audience member stumped me with a question. I said, "I'll need a moment. I want my answer to be useful to you." So I was not focused on "oh, I don't look perfect" – I was focused on thinking and forming a useful answer.

The powerful communicator focuses on giving goodness (love) to the audience. Be sure to focus on "How may I serve?"

Think about "how may I serve?" *Write in your journal* the ideas that can help you communicate more effectively.

* **A Side Note:** To replace fear on a consistent basis, consider devoting effort to healing. Perhaps, you might want to seek certain support groups, particular friends, a pet, a counselor, or a personal coach to help you gain the support you need.

Raise Your Self-Esteem and Improve Your Communication

Question #26: How can I raise my self-esteem?

Answer: Do you feel that you have value? How you rate yourself can deeply affect how you express yourself in front of other people. Several years ago, when I first began in the film industry, someone asked me whether I knew some prominent film industry person. I replied, "Not yet." My point of view is that people have intrinsic value. So if someone is prominent it is *not* because they are better. It means that they just have more experience and time to work at their trade.

Self-esteem is about two things: action and identity. Some people get into trouble about self-esteem because they only rate themselves based on their achievements. Here is a helpful definition:

"Self-esteem is the disposition to experience oneself as being competent to cope with the basic challenges of life and of being worthy of happiness. It is confidence in the efficacy of our mind, in our ability to think. By extension, it is confidence in our ability to learn, make appropriate choices and decisions, and respond effectively to change. It is also the experience that success, achievement, fulfillment – happiness – are right and natural for us." - Nathaniel Braden.

So it helps to focus on your ability to adapt, learn and flex (be flexible). I refer to these things with the mnemonic label "A.L.F."

Self-esteem and Action:

Sometimes you can do everything right and still you do not get the result you want. It helps your self-esteem to divide goals into Effort-Goals and Result-Goals.

Examples:

- Effort-Goal: Make 10 marketing phone calls per day
- Result-Goal: Gain one new client per week

When you fulfill your Effort-Goal, you can still feel worthy (higher self-esteem) even when results are not arriving as fast as you prefer.

Write in your journal some Effort-Goals and Result-Goals. Develop a system to take some action each day.

Self-esteem and Identity:

Some people only define themselves by their achievements and conventional roles (wife, friend, parent). What if a loved one is upset with you—what are you then? You can have a good measure of calm and inner peace when you support yourself by expanding your focus points for your identity. You can take an "eternal view." Here are examples:

- I am Higher Power's child.
- I am growing and learning.
- I am Spirit having a human experience
- I continually find loving ways to benefit others and myself.

Note your thoughts in your journal on this "identity" topic.

Peace and Contentment in the moment

When I'm doing a workshop, things can be hectic. Before some workshops, there may be a line of attendees who wish to talk with me. When possible, I invite the person to join me in sitting in chairs. Why? We can both take a breath and relax. At that point, I can really focus on the student seated before me. At times, I will tell myself: "I really appreciate this person in front of me."

Question #27: How do I bring more peace and

contentment into this moment?

Answer: Feeling peace results from your skillful use of Thoughts, Stories and Breathing. We will use the C.A.N. process:

C – Concentrate the "SwitchPhrase"

A – "Affirm-breathe"

N – Nurture stories

1. Concentrate the "SwitchPhrase"

Some people try to force themselves to step away from disquieting thoughts. They may tell themselves to "concentrate, concentrate!" We will use a more helpful process: the SwitchPhrase is a phrase you memorize to guide your thoughts into a positive direction.

Let's say it's Sunday and you are walking in a park. Worries about Monday are pushing you into the future and you're missing the healing effects of your walk. You could form a SwitchPhrase like: "Blue sky. Grass. Relaxed." As you repeat this phrase to yourself like a mantra, you can breathe deeply. You say "relaxed" as if it was a pre-existing fact as opposed to a command.

What "SwitchPhrase" that you form might help you calm down?

2. "Affirm-breathe"

One of my mentors suggested that I use deep-breathing to feel peaceful each day. She suggested breath-in while counting 1-2-3-4. Hold the breath for "1-2-". And then breathe out while internally counting 1-2-3-4-5-6-7-8." I did not find counting to be peaceful.

Instead, I choose to come up with an affirmation (a positive statement).

My clients have chosen affirmations including:

- God relaxes me.
- I am love.
- I am well.
- I'm grateful.

The process is that you repeat your affirmation for each part of the breathing exercise: breath-in, hold, breathe-out.

What affirmations would you like to use when you "Affirm-Breathe"?

3. Nurture stories

At the table where I type this is a sparkling Tiffany crystal bowl holding napkins. I won this bowl at a spiritual retreat. The story I tell myself is "I win things." This brings a smile to my face.

Now it's your turn. I invite you to search your past for positive stories. Tell these positive stories to yourself and others.

What are three positive stories that you can tell yourself (and others)?

Ensure You Have Energy to Make A Great First Impression

Question #28: How do you create more energy so you have it when you're making a first impression?

Answer: Devote focus to unleash energy from deep inside you. Listen to your Emotional Self and support it.

Some authors/researchers identify the Emotional Self as the Inner Child.

You gain the energy from the Inner Child by asking questions, writing your answers and then taking action. The idea is to support yourself and enhance your personal energy.

Questions for your Inner Child:
(Write your answers quickly; do not allow your rational mind to block your answers.)

- Inner Child, how are you feeling?
- Inner Child, is there something I can do for you so you feel better?
- Inner Child, what would you like to do?
- What would be fun?

You do not need to devote lots of time. A bit of time daily can do wonders. For example, for 15 minutes before I sat down to write this section, I listened to music and assembled a jigsaw puzzle. This alone-time recharges my battery. (Recharging one's "battery" is a useful process for an introvert.)

Will you devote ten minutes to writing down a "dialogue" with your Inner Child?

Gaining Energy through the Skillful Use of Food and Exercise

Question #29: How can I have lots of energy for networking events?

Answer: It helps to do two things:

- transform your relationship with food
- transform your relationship with exercise

1. Transform your relationship with food.

I have learned that it helps to develop a number of ways to comfort yourself. I have found the easiest thing is to watch TV (after a long work day) and eat snacks. I often *avoid* that!

So I've looked for ways to gain comfort without calories. Some people take a hot bath or a go for a walk.

In terms of having energy for a networking event, I eat before I attend the event. Then I do have the energy. But I eat some time before so that my physical resources are *not* tied up with digestion. I want to be sharp.

For example, I have given presentations at dinner meetings. And I eat *after* I've given my presentation.

What good decisions do you want to make about your interactions with food?

2. Transform your relationship with exercise.

I've learned to make exercise a natural part of my day. For example, I read everyday. I read while safely walking on my treadmill. Reading makes treadmill-time zoom by.

I keep a Progress Log of my daily exercise. For example, years ago, I had neck pain so I do neck exercises (recommended by physical therapists) everyday. Some time ago, I had my first back spasm. Now I do daily back exercises (recommended by physical therapists).

I do my neck exercises and back exercises while family members watch a TV show.

Researchers verify that daily exercise actually creates more energy for each person who completes such activity.

How can you make exercise a natural part of your day?

How can you take the pain/inconvenience out of your daily exercise routines?

Create Transcendent Moments

Question #30: How do I create Transcendent Moments?

Answer: Set the stage. Go to where you will feel refreshed. Many of us find a hike in nature to be invigorating. I enjoy going to Disney theme parks because I enjoy being immersed in all the refreshing creativity. I keep a notebook with me because I get inspired and write down new ideas and portions of books and graphic novels.

For example, to have refreshing moments with family, do your best to **rest up** before visiting elderly parents. One time, I rested up before visiting my mother while she was in the hospital (She is recovered now. Thank goodness!) Rested, I told her stories and got her to laugh and enjoy herself. The good connection with my mother felt like *transcendent moments.* She healed up and returned home from the hospital faster.

A twenty minute nap can do wonders.

Sometimes, I take a nap in the backseat of a car before I go to an event. Such a rest energizes me to be at my best in the public.

Actor/comedian Bob Hope was well-known for being able to nap on a helicopter and just about anywhere. He rested up and had lots of energy to entertain American soldiers wherever they were stationed.

Quiet Down Nervousness Before a Speech

Question #31: How can I quiet down nervousness before I give a speech?

Answer: Visit the audience members before your speech. You can say, "Hello, I'm ____. I'm your speaker for today. When you heard about my topic, what were you hoping I'd talk about? What topic would be helpful for you? [Do you have a particular question you'd like me to cover?]."

During the beginning of your speech, you can say, "I talked with a number of you before this presentation. Susan brought up an important topic ____ ____."

This process of visiting with audience members before your speech helps you to pre-set "friendly faces" in your audience. You start off with some warm connections.

What questions do you plan to ask when you meet people in your audience *before* you give a speech?

Feel Strong Before a Difficult Communication Situation

Question #32: What can I do to feel strong for difficult communication situations?

Answer: Rehearse and take care of your essential needs. If you're tired, hungry, lonely or stressed out it is hard to be at your best in a difficult communication situation.

Secondly, if you have not rehearsed, it is likely that the effective words will not flow out of your mouth with poise and confidence.

Any time you feel concern or even fear about an upcoming difficult communication situation, ask yourself: "Have I fulfilled my essential needs? Have I rehearsed?"

What actions will you take this week to fulfill your essential needs—and to rehearse?

Make Your Dreams Come True
How to Dust Off Your Dreams

Question #33: How can I "dust off" my dreams?

Answer: With clients, I often ask the question: "If the Genie from Aladdin was standing next to us, what would you wish for—if you could have it just by clearly saying what you want?"

The idea is to step out of so-called "realistic concerns."

Do *not* start with trying to be realistic.

Numerous highly accomplished people talk about working with what they have and new opportunities arriving as a result—opportunities that they did not imagine before.

For example, Vanessa Williams mentioned that she had not thought of applying to the Miss America Pageant. It was *not* her focus. What she wanted to do was to sing and act on Broadway. But then the opportunity arose and she took action.

When, for a time she could not get parts on Broadway, she discovered a surprise opportunity to sing pop-songs. She went forward with opportunities as they arose.

Every time I reach to accomplish something big, I just take steps forward. Currently, my team and I are completing graphic novels in the *Jack AngelSword* series. I currently do not know as many people in the graphic novel/comics industry as I want to. But I hold the faith that I will keep reaching out and my dream of *Jack AngelSword* serving many people will come true. My big dream is that *Jack AngelSword* will continue as a franchise beyond my lifespan. I hold to that dream and take steps forward daily.

What would you aim for if you knew you could not fail?

What heartfelt dream have you dismissed because you have not seen clearly how to step toward it?

What little action can you make toward your dream? (Perhaps, you could join a group on Linkedin.com related to your dream? Then you could pose a question to that group.)

Overcome Feeling Overwhelmed

Question #34: How can I stop feeling overwhelmed by my daily life and job—and have energy for my dream-job?

Answer: Focus on effective Self-Care Methods. They center on the 4 M's: Mind, Movement, Music, Meals.

What can you do to ease your mind? (Quiet time, meditation, prayer time, time reading sacred texts)

What can you do to increase movement in your daily life? (Taking a brief walk during lunchtime, riding a stationary bicycle when watching TV, taking a yoga class or tai chi class)

What can you do to enjoy music sometime in your day? (Create a "soothing playlist" for your iPod and/or create an "energizing playlist")

What can you do to improve your meals? (Pick an enjoyable salad dressing so you eat more salads . . . I eat salad at breakfast time because my willpower is stronger in the morning).

Success as the Progressive Realization of Worthy Goals*

* A quote by Earl Nightingale

Question #35: How can I feel successful?

Answer: Feeling successful relates to three things: a) your ability to focus on the present moment, b) how you set and achieve goals and c) how you think and feel about your identity.

We will use the P.E.N. process:

P – Pinpoint the present moment

E – Empower your goals

N – Nurture your empowered identity

1. Pinpoint the present moment

What are you doing now? Are you taking action to make things better? Or are you stuck ruminating over something that went wrong? If you're stuck with ruminating, you likely do not feel successful. Material success is a moving target. By this I mean, if you achieve an income goal then the human tendency is target a new, larger number. If you have written one book that sold 15,000 copies, then the tendency is to view the accomplishment as small compared to someone who has sold 3 million copies of her book.

Feeling successful only takes place in this moment and depends on your healthy focus. For example, I can feel successful when I recall how I have helped several people gain jobs. Has every audience member taken action based on my material? No. Some were going through tough times and they did not have the "space" to devote effort during my workshop or presentation.

My feeling successful depends on my healthy choices regarding what I focus on in this present moment.

Now it's your turn.

What can you focus on that reminds you of value you have created and helps you feel successful in this present moment?

2. Empower your goals

A number of people have real problems around setting goals. Some say they're not sure what they want.

You can start with:

What do you want to get better in your life?

What troublesome thing or painful thing do you want to stop?

If the Genie from Aladdin would simply give you what you want (do not think of how you have to work to get it), what would you wish for?

How would you feel better if you had the new thing, new opportunities or new experiences in your life?

Next, separate your goals into Effort-Goals (like making ten marketing phone call a day) and Result-Goals (gain two new clients each week). You can always be proud of yourself for completing your Effort-Goals.

Write down your Effort-Goals and Result-Goals.

3. Nurture your empowered identity

Do you define yourself by one certain result? That makes you vulnerable. The reality is: You can do everything right and still not gain the result you wanted.

Instead, you can feel successful when you set up your identity on some details that are *other* than your achievements.

Here are examples from clients:

- I am kind and friendly to people each day.
- I listen to people and that helps them feel better.
- I am growing and Higher Power is guiding me.
- Each day, I do some work related to my best talents and I am improving in my skills.

The above details do *not* rest on specific achievements. If you rest your identity on externals (achievements, physical appearance, comparing yourself with others), you are likely to hardly ever feel successful.

Instead, define your identify on details that you can appreciate about yourself and your life *in this present moment*.

Overcome Feeling Nervous On Meeting New People

Question #36: How can I handle nervousness when meeting new people?

Answer: Transform your focus from yourself (How am I doing?) to the other person (How are *you* doing?). Instead of trying to say something clever and attempt to impress the other person, show the person that you are *impressed* with him or her. Ask gentle questions (questions that are easy and even fun to answer).

You can ask:

- So how is the conference going for you?
- Are you looking forward to a particular speaker?
- What are you looking forward to?

As you listen carefully, ask follow up questions like:

- It sounds like you felt _____, and then what happened?
- That sounds like it was frustrating. How did you—?

Instead of trying to impress someone, you are helping the person feel good because he or she is being heard.

Self-Actualization

Question #37: How do I get to self-actualization?

Answer: Abraham Maslow defined *self-actualization* as "the desire for self-fulfillment, namely the tendency for him [the individual] to become actualized in what he is potentially. This tendency might be phrased as the desire to become more and more what one is, to become everything that one is capable of becoming."

Maslow emphasized that one needed to take care of one's basic needs and then a person could take care of one's higher needs—the pinnacle is self-actualization.

It's understandable that one needs to take care of his or her needs for food, shelter and companionship.

I have experienced that if one has a vision, it can help one endure tough situations in life.

I am enduring temporary sufferings to fulfill my dearest dreams. — Lailah Gifty Akita

While I was editing and directing my first feature film, I lived in an in-law apartment with wild rats chasing each other in the walls.

I worked at a job at a bank only to pay the rent at the time. So according to Maslow, I was covering my basic needs of food, shelter (such as it was) and companionship.

My "self-actualization focus point" on filmmaking empowered me to keep going.

He who has a why can endure any how. – Friedrich Nietzsche

What do you want deep in your heart and how might that empower you to endure temporary sufferings?

Create Closeness with Loved Ones

Question #38: How do I create closeness with people who are important to me?

Answer: Set up "Closeness-Rituals." Some couples play board games each week so they have fun together. Others have a conversation each week as they take their evening stroll.

One mother has a "Breakfast Ritual" in which she goes out to breakfast with her son each Saturday.

What form of Closeness-Ritual do you want to establish with someone you love?

Communicate Well and Develop a Team-Feeling

Question #39: How do I create a team-feeling?

Answer: Provide enough information so that each person sees and feels the value of team members' contributions.

For example, while my team completed my first graphic novel, *Crystal Pegasus,* I set up a private blog in which each completed page was posted. We had four colorists working on separate pages and all team members could see the contributions made by others in the group. This raised morale and kept us to a good schedule.

What will you do to show team members' contributions so that everyone on the team sees the progress and feels "we're all in this together"?

The Power of Forgiveness

Question #40: Where does forgiveness fit in with communication?

Answer: To communicate well and make a positive connection with people, it helps to let go of grudges and blame. For example, years ago, I endured a misunderstanding with "George." I did *not* hold a grudge nor did I "cut him off." Years later, he invited me to be a guest on his radio show.

I realized that at the time of the misunderstanding, George may have been under extra pressure and that is how the miscommunication occurred.

Make no judgments where you have no compassion.

– Anne McCaffrey

In one of my books, I wrote: "Forgiveness is not pardon; it's looking at the big picture." All of us buckle under strain at times. (I am **NOT** talking about enduring abuse. That calls for different actions including *getting away* from the person and more.)

To communicate well use **"I-language"** that sounds like this "I feel frustrated when I'm waiting..." Avoid "blame-language" that includes "You jerk! You don't care about me. You're always late."

In a situation where it's hard to forgive someone, see how you functioned in the situation. How did you participate in the situation? Do you need to assert yourself in a new way?

Is there a particular situation in which you need to forgive? What positive steps can you take?*

* Would it be helpful for you to learn more about forgiveness? I was a guest expert on a TV show with Dr. Fred Luskin as another guest expert. I appreciated when he said, "Forgiveness is choosing to end the cycle of blame and suffering." Fred's book, *Forgive for Good,* is helpful.)

Getting Yourself to Stretch and Grow

Question #41: How can I get myself to stretch?

Answer: Some authors refer to the Biblical quote "Where there is no vision, the people perish." (Proverbs 29:18)

I'll add my own thought: "With a vision, you'll have inner inspiration to strive for more and better."

In other words, you will do better when you have a strong connection to your personal purpose.

Some people have written complicated "mission statements" but such formal documents have gathered dust at the back of day planners and on a walls long hidden by clutter. It's better to have something brief that you can memorize and live!

For example, my Personal Mission Caption (brief, like words below a photograph) is: "I help people experience enthusiasm, love and wisdom to fulfill Big Dreams."

Write two versions of a Personal Mission Caption.

For my company I wrote the follow:

"We create energizing, encouraging edutainment for our good and humankind's rise." – Tom Marcoux Media, LLC Mission Statement

Write down three versions of a one sentence "caption" that expresses the uplifting purpose of your company or organization. [You can do this even if you work for someone else's company. Think of yourself as an operating unit inside that company. Have your own purpose and "mission caption."]

How You Can Jump Start Your Day

Question #42: How can I jump start my day?

Answer: Have something pull you out of bed. For some it may be writing for 20 minutes. I tend to write for a time before I have breakfast.

For others, it may be playing a guitar for 10 minutes. Have the guitar on a stand so you can just pick it up quickly.

Some people force themselves to exercise in the morning and dreading that task may have them setting the snooze alarm twice! Instead, have something you *want* to do to get you moving quickly in the morning.

Instead, have something you want to do to get you going.

When you get something done in the morning, you feel good because you have started the day with a Personal Victory.

Also consider this method: *Wake Up in Gratitude.*

Some of my clients arise with a first thought like:

- Thank you, Higher Power for this day.
- Thank you, God for this glorious day for love, prosperity and great health!

What will you implement that gives you a big pull to get up a bit earlier each morning?

How You Can Be Welcomed Wherever You Go

Question #43: How can I do something so I am welcomed wherever I go?

Answer: My mentor the late speaker/author Dottie Walters suggested that one observes carefully and then gives a person a sincere compliment. "That tells me something about you. You really held your calm during that disagreement a moment ago. That's great."

The plan is to provide a sincere compliment and you will brighten the other person's day.

What admirable qualities or actions have you observed in co-workers, friends or family members? How will you give them sincere compliments?

The Best Time and Way to Give Someone Your Business Card

Question #44: When is the best time to give someone my business card?

Answer: Be sure to have a meaningful and positive conversation *before* you hand out your business card. Even though people may be gathered for a networking event, they still bristle when someone is overbearing. They also cringe when it appears that someone is trying too hard to get something from them.

The solution is to have a conversation first and for you to listen at least 75% of the time. After an appropriate amount of time, you can say, "It's been great talking with you. And it would be good to stay in contact. Do you have a business card?"

It's strange, but about 65% of the time, the person does not have a business card. Then, you can say, "Oh, I can make one for you" as you pull out a 3x5 card from your pocket. You continue, "So are you at gmail or yahoo mail?"

I have noted that people feel comfortable to provide a gmail address or they'll simply give you another email address.

Finally, this is the time to say, "Oh, and I'll share my card with you." *That's* when you hand the person your business card.

Note: This is *opposite* of the person who acts like an overbearing used car salesperson who slams their card into everyone's hand.

Will you carry 3x5 cards so you can "make a business card" for those not carrying their business cards?

Will you rehearse the above process of conversation and exchanging business cards?

What Impresses People?

Question #45: How can I impress new people I have met?

Answer: *Respond quickly.* A number of people I have met will let days go by before replying to an email message. Not good.

Instead, do your best to respond quickly.

When interacting with team members at the university where I teach, I often provide filled out documents or other responses in the same day that someone makes a request.

Why? I want to have the outstanding reputation (personal brand) that the university personnel do *not* have to wait or worry about my getting back to them.

I have coached my interns to reply quickly even if they do not have a full answer yet. I've noticed some business people delay and wait a few days before they have a full answer to an email's query. Instead, I coach clients to respond as fast as possible with something like: "I received your email and I'm looking into this. I expect to have an answer for you on Thursday afternoon. How does this sound?"

One of my mentors said, "An email is a plea in the wilderness. Also, if someone has sent you a query, it is likely that they have sent the same email to other potential vendors. The person who responds quickly gets the business."

How will you change your habits so that you can respond quickly to people's questions, emails, and voicemails?

Inspire People to Trust You

Question #46: How do I inspire trust?

Answer: I invite my clients to develop a strong, positive personal brand. A good foundation is what I call T.H.O.R.: Trustworthy, Helpful, Organized, Respectful.

a) Trustworthy. Do you do what you promised? It's best to be careful with what you promise. Be a bit slow to say *yes*. Ask for time to think (I call this getting "thinkspace.") You could say, "I'll need to double check a couple of details. How about I get back to you about this on Thursday afternoon?"

b) Helpful. Many people are competent and effective at their jobs. Unfortunately, they radiate their self-focus and disdain for others. People will trust you when you demonstrate that you intend to be of service to them.

c) Organized. Someone may have good intentions but be unskillful at completing work well and on time. That will torpedo keeping clients or getting referrals.

Instead, be careful to avoid telling stories about yourself that imply incompetence. Instead, craft your stories to show how you come through for people.

d) Respectful. People simply want to continue working with those who make it a pleasure to do so. I have worked with some people who are grumpy and crude in their language. Some of my friends have left vendors who have particular gruff manners. They told me that those vendors made them feel uncomfortable and they looked for someone else to work with.

Instead, be sure to be polite and respectful and you're more likely to have continuing clients and more referrals.

How will you demonstrate to people that you are Trustworthy, Helpful, Organized and Respectful?

Getting Someone to Want to Listen to You

Question #47: How do I get someone to want to hear what I have to say?

Answer: Listen to the other person first. When two people meet together, often there is subtle tension as the other person wants his or her own opinion heard first. Let the other person have the floor. Ask, "Is there anything else?" so the person gets it all out. Then the other person feels more comfortable. Be sure to assure the person that you understood what they said. Say something like: "Mary, I heard you to say..." or "Mary, you want XYZ to be done. Is that about right?"

Once assured that she has been understood, the person will then ask you, "So what did *you* want to tell me?"

A number of people I have met will feel an obligation to reciprocate and listen. (Not all people reciprocate. But many do.)

Getting A Difficult Person to Listen to You

Question #48: How do I get someone who habitually does NOT listen to hear my idea?

Answer: Lead with the other person's words first. (The person is enamored with their own point of view.) It can sound like this. "Joe, last week you mentioned the XYZ process needs to start with the 1-2-3 steps. And I noticed that if we add ABC then it all works better."

How will you "quote" the person and get their attention?

Inspiration

Question #49: How about some inspiration?

Answer: I will provide three phrases I have written that help my clients move forward in life.

* To stand out, find out what you stand for.

(I've learned that when you find out what you value and you commit to improvement, then you can make an impact—that benefits others and yourself.)

* Keep score and achieve more.

(I have discovered that I can get myself to do something consistently when I keep score. I turn it into a positive game. I keep a Progress Log of my exercise. Sometimes, I'm just about to go to sleep, but then I look at my exercise log and note that I forgot to do my back exercises and neck exercises—so I make sure to get them done before the end of my day.)

* Small steps bring surprise leaps.

(I have observed that a small step leads to another step and momentum builds. I gave a speech that led to writing a book and that led to giving a class on technical communication. From there, I gave workshops at Stanford University to MBA students. That was a positive surprise!)

Question #50: Tell me something about success.

Answer: Here are some useful principles.

"Successful people ask questions. They seek new teachers. They're always learning." - Robert Kiyosaki

After enduring a time of desperation when I first aimed to raise funds to make a feature film, I've learned to study every day. I tend to read 81 books per year.

How will you get new information? (Books, coaches, video training?)

"A professional is someone who can do his best work when he doesn't feel like it." - Alistair Cooke

When it's time to write, I do not wait to feel inspired or even to feel good. I simply sit down and start typing. Often, I do not feel good for the first five minutes. I just keep working and better work emerges. When it's time for me to draw a first draft of a graphic novel page, I tell my illustrator, "I'll call you back in 15 minutes," and I sketch the page. No hesitation. I know we can fix the page in later revisions.

What do you value enough so that you will push yourself past a bad mood in order to get some progress done?

"Inspiration usually comes during work rather than before it."
– Madeleine L'Engle

Author Malcolm Gladwell emphasized research, revealing that 10,000 hours of practicing a specific task can bring one to world-class levels of work. By writing 26 books, I developed my skills so that I can write better. I have also learned from each of my editors. I have practiced numerous ways to solve writing challenges. Using these methods allows me to break through stuck-points.

What do you want so much that you're willing to devote some daily efforts?

A FINAL WORD AND
THE SPRINGBOARD TO YOUR DREAMS

Congratulations on your efforts with this book. Thank you for your attention. When you return to these pages again and again, you can *reenergize yourself*. You will get more value each time you review the steps covered in this book.

To gain more value and use this book as a springboard, be sure to go through it and note your new tasks *in your calendar*. Take some action. Any action towards improving skills and enlarging your life is helpful. I often say, "Better than zero."

* * *

Please consider gaining special training through my

coaching (phone and in-person), workshops, presentations and Top Five Group Elite Video Training. My coaching features innovations: *Dynamic Rehearsal* and *Power Rehearsal for Crisis*. Due to my background in improvisation and training in acting, directing and screenwriting, I help clients *as I improvise dialogue* during rehearsal sessions. I coach clients to prepare for speeches and any tough or vital conversation with audiences, colleagues, sales prospects and even family members.

As you continue to work toward expanding your financial abundance and fulfillment in life, you are likely to come up against some tough situations. To be supportive I've written a number of books . . .

- Darkest Secrets of Charisma
- Darkest Secrets of Persuasion and Seduction Masters: How to Protect Yourself and Turn the Power to Good
- Darkest Secrets of Negotiation Masters
- Darkest Secrets of Making a Pitch to the Film and Television Industry
- Darkest Secrets of Film Directing
- Darkest Secrets of the Film and Television Industry Every Actor Should Know
- Darkest Secrets of Spiritual Seduction Masters
- Success Secrets of Rich, Smart and Powerful People: How You Can Use Leverage for Business Success

See my blog at
www.BeHeardandBeTrusted.com

The best to you,
Tom
Tom Marcoux,
America's Communication Coach, TFG Thought Leader,

Spoken Word Strategist
Motion Picture Director, Actor, Producer, Screenwriter
P.S. See **Free Chapters** of Tom Marcoux's 26 books
at http://amzn.to/ZiCTRj   (at Amazon.com)

Titles include:
Be Heard and Be Trusted
Nothing Can Stop You This Year
Truth No One Will Tell You
Yes! Secrets for Your Best Life . . . Law of Attraction . . .
Reduce Clutter, Enlarge Your Life
Power Time Management   — and more.
(For coaching, reach Tom Marcoux
 at tomsupercoach@gmail.com)

EXCERPT FROM
DARKEST SECRETS OF PERSUASION AND SEDUCTION MASTERS: HOW TO PROTECT YOURSELF AND TURN THE POWER TO GOOD

by Tom Marcoux, America's Communication Coach
Copyright Tom Marcoux

. . . Now, I am in my 40's, with gray in my hair, and for 27 years I have been taking action to protect people.

And now is the time for me to protect you with the Countermeasures I reveal in this book.

Every human being needs to be able to
break the trance that a Manipulator creates.
You need to make good decisions
so you are safe and you keep growing
—and you are not cut down and crippled.

This Darkest Secrets material is so intense that I first released it only with the counterbalance of my most energizing and uplifting books, *Nothing Can Stop You This Year!* and *10 Seconds to Wealth: Master the Moment Using Your Divine Gifts.*

An interviewer asked me: "Who can be the Manipulator?"

A co-worker, a boss, a salesperson, someone you're dating, and someone you think is a friend.

Now is the time—this very minute—for me to write this book to protect you.

I must speak the truth.

These Darkest Secrets of "persuasion masters" are ...

Wait a minute! Let's say it plainly: These are the Darkest Secrets of masters of manipulation. Throughout this book, I will call these people what they are: Manipulators.

Dictionary.com defines "manipulate" as "To influence or manage shrewdly or deviously.... To tamper with or falsify for personal gain."

In this book, we will look on a manipulator as one who deviously influences someone with no concern about that person's well-being, and who causes harm to that person.

Here is the first Darkest Secret:

Darkest Secret #1:

Manipulators Make You Hurt

and Then Offer the Salve.

Manipulators would invite you to go out in the sun for hours and then sell you the salve to soothe your burns. The problem is that we don't notice that this is what they're doing.

For example, you're considering the purchase of a house. A Manipulator asks the question, "So, where would you put your TV?" This question is designed to put you into a trance.

Dictionary.com defines "trance" as "a half-conscious

state, seemingly between sleeping and waking, in which ability to function voluntarily may be suspended." Let's condense this: in a trance you may not be able to function freely.

Here is the second Secret:

Darkest Secret #2:

Manipulators Put You into a Trance.

To protect yourself, you must learn to use Countermeasures to Break the Trance.

All the Countermeasures (actions you can take to break the trance) in this book will make you stronger and more capable of protecting yourself.

Now, we'll view the third Secret:

Darkest Secret #3:

Manipulators Care Nothing for You and Human Decency: They'll lie, cheat, and do whatever they need to do so they win—but their charm masks all this.

Let's return to the example of a Manipulator selling you a house. A Manipulator does not pause for an instant to see if you can truly afford the new house. The Manipulator would neglect to mention that you will not only have your mortgage payment of $900. There will be additional costs: home repairs, property tax, water, electricity, homeowner's insurance, and more. The Manipulator only emphasizes what he or she knows you want to hear: "Look! $900 is better than the $1500 you're paying for rent, which is just going down the toilet. And the $900 is an investment."

Let's go back to **Darkest Secret #1:**

Manipulators make you hurt and then offer the salve.

The Manipulator has you feeling good about the solution (salve) and feeling bad about your current life situation.

How? A Manipulator will make you hurt through questions such as:

• What bothers you about paying $1500 a month for rent? (The Manipulator will use a derisive tone when he says the word rent.)

• What is not smart about paying rent on someone else's house instead of investing in your own house?

• How do you feel about your children walking in the neighborhood where you live now?

Do you see how these questions are designed to make you hurt enough so that you'll buy?

An interviewer asked me, "Tom, aren't these good arguments for purchasing a house?"

"What we're looking at is the *intention* of the influencer," I replied. "Let's look at our definition of a manipulator as one who deviously influences someone with no concern about that person's well-being, and who causes harm to that person. If the person truly cannot afford the house, he or she will be harmed by buying it. If the manipulator conceals the truth, the manipulator is doing harm. That's the important difference."

Some friends of mine are ethical and helpful real estate agents who truthfully reveal the whole situation and help the purchaser achieve her own goals.

In this book, we are talking about another type of person; that is, unethical Manipulators.

* * *

In any given moment, we need to remember the tactics Manipulators use. We will focus on the word D.A.R.K. so you can remember details easily and protect yourself from Manipulators.

D — Dangle something for nothing

A — Alert to scarcity

R — Reveal the Desperate Hot Button

K — Keep on pushing buttons

1. Dangle Something for Nothing

What do conmen and conwomen do to seize your attention? They make you think you're getting a "steal."

I recently saw a documentary in which a conman on a street in England showed a toy that looked like it was dancing. This fake product was actually dancing because of a hidden, invisible thread. The conman was dangling something for nothing. The Entranced Buyer thought he was getting something worth $20 for only $5. That was the trick. The Entranced Buyer felt that he was getting $15 extra of value for his $5. What the Buyer really got was something worth nothing. Similarly, I know someone who purchased a copy of a Disney movie from a street vendor in San Francisco. She brought the copy home and it was unwatchable—and the street vendor was never seen again.

An old phrase goes, "A conman cannot con someone who is not looking for something for nothing."

How to Protect Yourself from "Dangle Something for Nothing"

Stop! Get on your cell phone and talk through the "deal" with someone you know who thinks clearly. Go home. Think about it. Do some research on the Internet. Listen to your gut feelings. If the salesman or conman is too insistent, get away from that Manipulator. Get quiet. Have a cup of water. Cool down. Break the Trance!

Break the Trance and Identify the Crucial Detail

Earlier, I mentioned that a Manipulator puts you into a

trance. An added problem is that we put ourselves into a trance. For example, as you read this, are you thinking about your right toe? Most likely not (unless you stubbed your toe recently). The point is that we only focus on a tiny percentage of what is going on in our life.

Around fifteen years ago, I caused myself trouble because I put myself into a trance. I discovered that under certain conditions, friendship can make you nearly deaf. Here's how: I was producing a song for a motion picture. A good friend was singing backup in the chorus. Because of our friendship, I wanted him to sound great. I completely missed the Crucial Detail. In this kind of situation, the Crucial Detail is that what truly counts is how the lead singer sounds! I made a song that I could not release. What a waste of time and money! I had put myself into a trance.

In any situation in which the Manipulator is "dangling something for nothing," we often fall into a trance and miss the Crucial Detail. The most important detail is *not* that we're saving money if we order before midnight tonight. What counts is whether the product creates a lasting, crucial benefit in our lives. And is the benefit of the product worth the cost? Some people even program themselves to make mistakes by saying, "I can't pass up a bargain." The bargain is *not* the Crucial Detail.

Secrets to Break the Trance

This is the process of B.R.E.A.K.S. It will help you remember the proven methods to break a trance.

B — Breathe

R — Relax

E — Envision

A — Act on aromas

K — Keep moving

S — Smile

Secret #1: Breathe

Remember Secret #1: Manipulators make you hurt and then offer the salve. The Manipulator wants to put you into a state of being that fills you with a sense of urgency and anxiety. Oh, no! I'm going to miss the sale!

Stop this highly vulnerable state. Take a deep breath. Do it now. Take a deep breath and let your belly "get fat" by filling it with air. As you breathe out, let your belly deflate. Breathe in through your nose and breathe out through your mouth. This is called belly-breathing. Repeat the actions of belly-breathing three times. Good. Now, do you feel different? Remember, when you are relaxed, you are strong.

End of Excerpt from
*DARKEST SECRETS OF PERSUASION AND
SEDUCTION MASTERS: HOW TO PROTECT
YOURSELF AND TURN THE POWER TO GOOD*
Copyright Tom Marcoux Media, LLC

Purchase your copy of this book (paperback or ebook) at Amazon.com or BarnesandNoble.com
See **Free Chapters** of Tom Marcoux's 26 books
at http://amzn.to/ZiCTRj

ABOUT THE AUTHOR

Tom Marcoux helps people like you fulfill big dreams. Known as America's Communication Coach and TFG Thought Leader, Tom has authored 26 books with sales in 15 countries. One of his *Darkest Secrets* books rose to #1 on Amazon.com Hot New Releases in Business Life (and in Business Communication). He guides clients and audiences (IBM, Sun Microsystems, etc.) to success in job interviewing, public speaking, media relations, and branding. A member of the National Speakers Association, he is a professional coach and guest expert on TV, radio, and print, and was dubbed "the Personal Branding Instructor" by the *San Francisco Examiner.* **Tom is the Spoken Word Strategist.**

Tom addressed National Association of Broadcasters' Conference six years running. With a degree in psychology, Tom is a guest lecturer at **Stanford University**, DeAnza, & California State University, and teaches public speaking, science fiction cinema/literature and comparative religion at Academy of Art University. Winner of a special award at the **Emmys**, Tom wrote, directed, and produced a feature film that the distributor took to the **Cannes film market**, and the film gained international distribution. He is engaged in book/film projects *Crystal Pegasus* (children's) and *TimePulse* (science fiction). See TomSuperCoach.com and Tom's well-received blog

at www.BeHeardandBeTrusted.com

Tom Marcoux can help you with **speech writing** and **coaching for your best performance.**

As Tom says, *Make Your Speech a Pleasant Beach.*

Join Tom's Linkedin.com group: *Executive Public Speaking*

and Communication Power.

At Google+: join the community "Create Your Best Life – Charisma & Confidence"

Get a **Free** report: "9 Deadly Mistakes to Avoid for Your Next Speech and 9 Surefire Methods" at

http://tomsupercoach.com/freereport9Mistakes4Speech.html

Tom Marcoux has trained CEOs, small business owners, and graduate students to speak with impact and gain audiences' tremendous approval and cooperation. *Learn how to present and get thunderous applause!*

"Tom, Thanks for your coaching and work with me on revising my speech at a major university. Working with you has been so enlightening for me. Through your gentle prodding and guidance I was able to write a speech that connects with the audience. I wish everyone could experience the transformation I have undergone. You have helped me discover the warm and compelling stories that now make my speech reach hearts and uplift minds. This was truly an empowering experience. I cannot thank you enough for your great assistance." — J.S.

"Tom Marcoux has been an NAB Conference favorite [speaker] for six years. And he is very energetic."
– John Marino,
Vice President, National Association of Broadcasters,
Washington, D.C.

"Using just one of Tom Marcoux's methods, I got more done in 2 weeks than in 6 months."
– Jaclyn Freitas, M.A.

Tom's Coaching features innovations:
* Dynamic Rehearsal

- Power Rehearsal for Crisis
- The Charisma Advantage that Saves Time

Become a fan of Tom's graphic novels/feature films:
Fantasy Thriller: *Jack AngelSword*
type "JackAngelSword" at Facebook.com

Science fiction: *TimePulse*
www.facebook.com/timepulsegraphicnovel

Children's Fantasy: *Crystal Pegasus*
www.facebook.com/crystalpegasusandrose

See **Free Chapters** of Tom Marcoux's 26 books
at http://amzn.to/ZiCTRj

Special Offer Just for Readers of this Book:
Contact Tom Marcoux at tomsupercoach@gmail.com for special discounts on books, coaching, workshops and presentations. Just mention your experience with this book.

www.ingramcontent.com/pod-product-compliance
Lightning Source LLC
Chambersburg PA
CBHW071657200326
41519CB00012BA/2544